FARM ANATOMY
ACTIVITIES FOR KIDS
Fun, Hands-On Learning

DAWN ALEXANDER, MS

ILLUSTRATIONS BY TARA SUNIL THOMAS

ROCKRIDGE
PRESS

For general information on our other products and services or to obtain technical support, please contact our Customer Care Department within the United States at (866) 744-2665, or outside the United States at (510) 253-0500.

Rockridge Press publishes its books in a variety of electronic and print formats. Some content that appears in print may not be available in electronic books, and vice versa.

Series Designers: Jane Archer and Karmen Lizzul
Interior and Cover Designer: Karmen Lizzul
Art Producer: Sara Feinstein
Editor: Elizabeth Baird
Production Editor: Ashley Polikoff

Illustrations © 2020 Tara Sunil Thomas. All other art used under license from © The Noun Project. Author photo courtesy of Arkansas Farm Bureau

ISBN: Print 978-1-64739-982-5 | eBook 978-1-64739-983-2
R0

CONTENTS

THIS WAS MADE ON A FARM

Have you ever thought about where the foods you eat or the clothes you are wearing come from? Your first thought might be, "Yes, they come from the store." And in a way, you are correct. But that's not where all of it begins. Have you heard of the word *agriculture*? Agriculture is the industry that grows plants and raises animals to bring us farming, food, fiber, fishing, forestry, and flowers. These are called the "six Fs of agriculture." Agriculture is everywhere, and it connects us all together. It's where almost everything we eat and use in our daily lives comes from.

Farming is the first step in making every kind of food you eat. Everything in your pizza, hamburger, or cookie starts as a seed or an animal that is grown, watered, fed, protected, and cared for by people. Then you have fish, which are farmed from oceans and rivers. Flowers are grown in nurseries. Timber is chopped from trees in forests and used to make paper and wood for our homes. Animal fiber, such as the wool or hair of sheep and goats, and plant fiber, such as cotton, are raised and grown on farms and used to make clothes, blankets, and carpet. All of this makes up agriculture.

This book teaches you about the plants and animals that are typically found on a farm. You'll learn where many of your favorite things come from. For example, did you know that crayons are made with soybeans and corn is used to make toothpaste? Even footballs, basketballs, baseballs, and tennis balls start on the farm. Their leather comes from cattle, and their rubber comes from trees!

You'll also learn about the people involved in agriculture, such as farmers and ranchers, who grow the plants and raise the animals that you'll learn about in this book. Today, one farmer or rancher can feed over 160 people! This makes them important for all of us. They not only make everything we need to live but also teach us important lessons about commitment, sustainability, hard work, innovation, and more.

The interactive lessons and activities in this book will help you think more like a farmer and understand how nature, farming, food, and animals shape the way you live. Let's go over different parts of the book so we can start your adventure in farming and ranching!

HOW TO USE THIS BOOK

There are 20 lessons in this book, each about a different part of agriculture. Each lesson is paired with an activity and journal exercise that will inspire you to ask questions, test your skills, and reflect on what you've learned. The lessons are all designed to help you use the skills that farmers and ranchers use every day as they work.

LESSONS

Each lesson teaches you about important ideas and elements in agriculture. You will learn interesting facts about popular plants and animals, where they live, how they grow, and how they are cared for. The lessons guide you step-by-step toward a learning goal and prepare you to test that goal in an activity.

ACTIVITIES

Activities are fun and exciting. They will challenge you to apply what you are learning in the lessons. Some activities are like science experiments. Others are arts and crafts projects. All have easy-to-follow instructions and tips to help you if you get stuck. Each activity also has a list of materials you'll need to get started. An adult can help you get the items in the list and swap them out for other things when needed. Be sure to pay close attention when you see the "Safety First" tips! These are important notes of caution and advice for completing the activity safely.

JOURNAL ENTRIES

After each lesson and activity, you will be prompted to write about what you are learning in a journal. You can use any type of notebook or paper—even a computer or tablet—to write down your observations. The journal sections will ask questions to guide your writing. You can copy these questions into your journal and write the answers beneath each one. You can also come up with your own questions about the activity. Write down these questions and answer them in the journal, too.

THE ANATOMY OF A FARM

Farms are homes to many plants and animals. And just like your home has rooms for eating and different rooms for sleeping, farms also have different areas that serve different purposes.

Think about the different things that you need to live—water, food, and shelter. Plants and animals need the same things, and farms are designed to provide for these different needs.

A dairy farm, for example, needs a place to milk cows every day. A cattle ranch needs space for cattle to graze. And a plant nursery (yet another type of farm) needs large greenhouses. This chapter guides you through different types of farms and helps you understand what farmers and ranchers need to take care of plants and animals.

WHERE DO FARM ANIMALS LIVE?

Apiculture

Aquaculture

Dairy

An animal farm is an area of land that is used to raise animals, and there are many different types, depending on the sort of animal being raised. Let's take a look at five types of animal farms.

Apiculture: This is another word for bee-keeping. Farmers who raise bees are called beekeepers. Many bees make honey and bees-wax. They also help crop farmers pollinate plants (pollination is the way that insects help plants make seeds). Beekeepers sometimes rent their bees to crop farmers for pollination.

Aquaculture: Aquaculture farms raise things like fish, shellfish, and aquatic plants for food and products. Freshwater aquaculture includes cat-fish, trout, and other organisms found in bodies of water that do not have salt in them. Marine aquaculture farms oysters, mussels, clams, shrimp, seaweed, and other saltwater life from the ocean.

Dairy: These farms raise animals that produce milk, which can be made into cheese, yogurt, butter, and other dairy products. Most dairy farms have cows, but some dairy farms raise sheep and goats for milk. All female dairy animals lactate, which means they produce milk, after giving birth.

Livestock: Livestock are farm animals that are raised for food or fiber. These include sheep, goats, rabbits, pigs, cattle, bison, llamas, and alpacas. They are usually kept in pens or large pastures, which are areas closed off by a fence. These animals are fed by farmers or ranchers.

Poultry: These farms raise chickens, turkeys, ducks, geese, and other birds (such as emus and ostriches) for meat, eggs, and feathers. Chickens are the most popular. Chickens raised for their eggs are called layers, and chickens raised for their meat are called broilers.

Now that you have learned about different types of farms, let's look at what these farms need in order to take care of animals. Animals, like humans, need comfortable places to live. These places on a farm are called shelters. Some animals, like cows, do well outside year-round in the right climate. They use trees for shade and protection from cold snow and rain. Other farm animals need to live in warm and dry places, like barns and sheds.

Barns: Barns are shelters that can be big like a house. In addition to protecting animals from the rain, wind, and cold, some barns also have space to store animal food, like hay.

Coops: Chickens live in special shelters called coops. These protect chickens from raccoons, skunks, owls, and other predators, and are comfortable homes in which they lay eggs and roost, or sleep.

Livestock

Poultry

Sheds: Other farms have shelters called sheds, which are usually smaller than a barn. These are usually open on all sides and have a roof to keep hay dry from rain and snow. Sheds are also used like garages to protect farm machines. Small farm animals such as pigs, sheep, and calves can use sheds as their home.

Animals, just like us, also need places to eat. These are called *feeding and grazing areas*. Cattle, sheep, and goats get their food from grass fields called pastures. In the winter, farmers and ranchers feed them hay. Pigs and chickens use smaller feeders to eat grain from. Farm animals also need special vitamins and minerals to help them grow stronger. These are kept in special containers that keep out the rain. Farmers also keep grains in tall, round metal towers called silos.

Fun Fact

Many farms, like the one in *The Wizard of Oz*, have windmills. Windmills have sails or vanes that are moved by the wind in circles. This movement produces energy. Windmills can use the energy from the wind to pump water for animals.

BUILD A BIRDHOUSE

TIME:
1 HOUR

CATEGORY:
CREATIVE, DESIGN AND BUILD

MATERIALS:
HALF-GALLON MILK CARTON,
WASHED AND DRIED COMPLETELY

PEN OR PENCIL

BOX CUTTER OR SCISSORS

NEWSPAPER (OPTIONAL)

COLORED MARKERS OR ACRYLIC
CRAFT PAINTS

NAIL

TWINE OR YARN

TIPS

➡ When drawing the door, make sure you leave some space around the edges. This will keep the house stable.

➡ If you want to turn your birdhouse into a birdfeeder, place some birdseed in the bottom of the carton.

You just learned that a barn can be a house where animals sleep and eat and also a place where farmers keep animal food, tools, and supplies. In this activity, you will build a birdhouse to provide a shelter to nearby birds with materials you can find in your home. A milk carton, for example, is already a great shape for a house—the top of the carton is like a pitched roof! Use your creativity to make your birdhouse unique.

Safety First: *Ask an adult to use a box cutter or scissors to cut the milk carton for you.*

INSTRUCTIONS

1. On one of the tall sides of the milk carton, use the pen to draw a rectangle or circle near the middle. This is the door the birds will use to get inside the house. Ask an adult to use the box cutter to cut out your shape.

2. If desired, lay down newspapers on a work surface to protect against spills. Use the colored markers or paints to decorate the birdhouse. If you're using paint, allow the paint to dry.

3. Use the nail to poke a hole on each side of the top of the milk carton.

4. Thread the twine through the two holes and make a knot at the top. This is how you will hang your birdhouse. Hang your birdhouse outside and watch the birds come and enjoy their new structure.

CONCLUSION:
Barns are one of the many structures on a farm. They are one of the places where animals live and can be protected from severe weather. In this activity, you built a shelter for birds, which protects them from the weather.

FARM JOURNAL ENTRY

Birdhouses are places for birds to build nests and have their young. They are also places for birds to keep dry and safe from severe weather. Use these questions to write about your birdhouse in your journal.

1. *What types of birds might live in your birdhouse?*

2. *Compare your birdhouse to your home. How are they similar? How are they different?*

3. *What are some ways you could improve the birdhouse to make it even more comfortable for the birds?*

WHERE DO CROPS GROW?

A crop is a plant or fruit that is grown to make food, clothes, and other products. Most crops are grown outside on large pieces of land, which are measured in units called **acres**. One acre is roughly the size of a football field. Like people, who live in different types of houses and in different places, crops grow in different environments.

Think about the things that grow around where you live. What is the weather like where you live? Does it get really hot in the summer? Does it snow in the winter? Farmers decide what crops to grow based on where they live, the type of soil, and the climate.

Let's look at a few vegetables and fruits that you probably like to eat. This table shows different types of crops, where they are grown in the United States, and what the climate is like there. What kind of crops grow best where you live?

Popular Crops and Where They Grow

CROP	TOP GROWING AREAS	CLIMATE AND SOIL
Bananas	Florida and Hawaii (but most are imported from Ecuador and Guatemala)	Tropical; 76°F to 86°F; rich, well-drained soil (but will grow in most soil types)
Corn	Heartland states, such as Illinois, Indiana, Iowa, Minnesota, and Nebraska	Warm, sunny weather; moderate rains; 130 frost-free days; rich, well-drained, sandy loam
Oranges	Arizona, California, Florida, and Texas	55°F to 100°F; light soil with good drainage
Potatoes	Colorado, Idaho, North Dakota, Washington, and Wisconsin	Cool to mild, not hot, weather; 70 to 90 cool days; soil that is well-drained and high in organic matter
Strawberries	California, Florida, North Carolina, Pennsylvania, and Wisconsin	Plenty of sunlight; 60°F to 80°F; soil rich in organic matter

Crops produce the most in regions where the growing conditions best suit their needs. As you can see in the table, banana trees grow well in tropical places, where the weather is warm and wet. Root plants like potatoes grow best in cool weather climates. If the climate is too hot, potatoes do not grow as well. The United States produces the most corn in the entire world, but corn is grown on every continent except Antarctica! However, not every country can produce every type of crop. Countries depend on being able to buy food they cannot grow from countries where it thrives. This is global trade.

Farmers can also change the natural growing conditions of the area around them. They might irrigate, or add water artificially, to soil when there is not enough rain. They add fertilizer to soil that does not have enough nutrients to produce healthy crops. Farmers also grow crops in greenhouses. The greenhouse traps the sun's heat to make growing conditions inside warmer than outside.

Fun Fact

Have you ever wondered why you can eat fresh blueberries with your yogurt in December? Your country likely buys blueberries from countries with warm Decembers, like those in South and Central America, so you can eat them in winter.

PLANTING CROPS WITHOUT SOIL

TIME:
30 TO 45 MINUTES ON DAY 1,
THEN 10 TO 15 MINUTES FOR
THE NEXT 8 TO 9 DAYS

CATEGORY:
EXPERIMENT,
OBSERVATION, PLANTS

MATERIALS:
WHEAT GRAINS

WATER

GLASS JAR OR RIMMED PLATE,
SUCH AS A PIE PLATE

SCISSORS

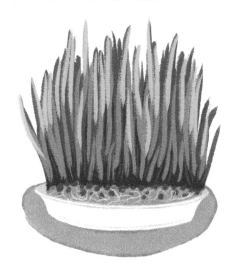

TIPS

➡ You can get wheat grain at garden centers or most health food stores. The amount you need depends on how big your glass jar or plate is. You need enough to cover the bottom of your container.

➡ Try planting wheatgrass seeds in soil and observe how they grow.

Most crops need sun, air, water, and soil in order for the plant to grow, but farmers and scientists have found new ways to grow plants without soil. One way is called hydroponics, which is growing plants so that they get food from water—without soil. Let's plant wheatgrass seeds and see what happens!

Safety First: *To harvest the wheatgrass, you will need a pair of scissors. Be careful when cutting and let an adult know you are using scissors.*

INSTRUCTIONS

1. Soak the wheat grains overnight in fresh, cold water.

2. The next day, pour off the water. Rinse the soaked grains well with water and drain them again.

3. Spread the grains out evenly in the glass jar or plate.

4. Continue to rinse and drain the grains well once or twice a day for several days. After about four to five days, your wheatgrass will begin to grow. The root hairs will look feathery; they are not mold. As long as you continue to rinse the grains, there should be no problem with mold.

5. After about six days of rinsing and draining, the leafy parts of the wheatgrass will appear.

6. After about eight days of rising and draining, your wheatgrass can be harvested! Just use scissors to cut close to the seeds. The wheatgrass will continue to grow like grass in someone's yard, so you can continue to harvest as you wish!

FARM JOURNAL ENTRY

Planting seeds is a fun way to learn about plant growth. Use these questions to write about your experience with planting wheatgrass seeds in your journal.

1. *Describe the steps the plant takes to get food from the water. How does that compare with plants that are grown in soil?*

2. *What would you do differently if you were to do this activity again?*

3. *Draw a picture of your wheatgrass plant each day to record the changes in the plant.*

CONCLUSION:
In the lesson you learned about where some crops grow and what farmers need to think about when planting their crops. Plants can grow in different environments, and in the activity, you planted a crop that can grow in water without soil. However, soil gives crops nutrients to help them grow, so wheatgrass grown in water will have fewer nutrients than wheatgrass grown in soil.

FARMING TOOLS AND MACHINES

Tools can improve a farmer's *efficiency*, or their ability to work without wasting time, energy, or money. When you have to write a paper using a pencil rather than a computer, the pencil requires more time and energy than the computer for you to complete your task. The principle of time-saving farm technologies is the same.

Agriculture has existed for a long time, as far back as ancient Egypt. Archeologists have found tools that the ancient Egyptians and other people throughout history have used to farm. Over time, people have invented ways to do the work easier, faster, and better. By observing the tools, you can see how farming technology has evolved throughout the years.

For example, ancient Egyptians used a type of plow that helped them plant seeds in the soil. It was pushed by hand and opened the earth. Later, when people were trying to farm in tougher soils, a different type of wooden plow was invented that could churn up the soil and loosen it enough for planting. Later still, the plow was redesigned so that animals, instead of people, could pull the plow; then farmers learned how to improve the plow's function by making it with different materials, and so on.

The History of
THE PLOW

Ancient Egyptian plow   A plow pulled by a horse   Modern-day tractor

When farmers had to plow a field by hand, it took about 96 hours, or four days, for the farmer to plow one acre, which is about the size of a football field. When the wooden plow was redesigned to be pulled using oxen or horses, that cut the farmer's time down to just 24 hours, or one day, for that acre. In 1837, a man named John Deere improved the plow by making it with steel, so it could handle the black prairie soil of the American Midwest. Now a farmer could go out and plow that acre in five to eight hours! Why was it so much faster? In the past, sticky soil would cling to the cast-iron plow blade, so the farmer would have to stop and clean it every few feet. Steel, on the other hand, is a slick metal, and the soil would not stick to the blades.

Today, plows with multiple moldboards—the main part that turns over the soil to loosen it—can plow several rows at once, which means a farmer can plow 50 acres (69 football fields) in one day. The plows are also pulled by tractors, which is another technology that has developed over the years. Recall that, before tractors were invented in the 1890s, oxen and horses were used to help the farmer in the field. It's tough work, and expending all that energy meant the farmers and animals had to rest. The work took so long that it limited how much food farmers could grow. Most people could only grow enough food to feed their families, and growing and harvesting that food took up all of their time.

Fun Fact

A tractor that a farmer uses today can help grow enough food to feed not just the farmer's own family but also 160 other people every year.

By the early 1900s, gas-powered tractors were becoming more popular among farmers. These tractors were mechanical and didn't need to rest like the farmers and horses did, and the tractors were faster all around. This helped farmers grow more food more efficiently. The tractor has continued to evolve to this day. For example, modern tractors are built to help reduce the impact of machinery in the fields so they are better for the environment, they cover more ground with each trip up and down the field, and they are equipped with computer technology to help the farmer apply just the right amount of seed and chemicals. It is predicted that in the future, there will be driverless tractors!

DESIGN AND BUILD A TRACTOR

TIME:
1 HOUR

CATEGORY:
CREATIVE, DESIGN AND BUILD

MATERIALS:
HALF-GALLON MILK CARTON, WASHED AND DRIED WELL

HALF-PINT MILK CARTON, WASHED AND DRIED WELL

TAPE OR GLUE

ACRYLIC PAINT OR MARKERS

PLASTIC LIDS OR BOTTLE CAPS (4)

EMPTY PAPER TOWEL OR TOILET PAPER ROLL

ALUMINUM FOIL

SCISSORS

TIP

➡ Draw your design in your journal before you start building. To test the functionality of your tractor, design something for it to pull and a hitch to pull it with. What will the hitch be made of?

In this activity, you will use your innovation skills to design and build a tractor, just like early farmers designed and built tools to help them farm. Use materials you find around your house, such as those listed here, to build your model. However, these are just suggestions; use your creativity to find what works. Try to design your tractor so that it is able to pull things behind it, just like tractors on a farm. It may take more than one try to get it right!

Safety First: *You may want to use hot glue to attach the milk cartons. An adult will need to help you with this part.*

INSTRUCTIONS

1. Look at pictures of tractors and use your imagination and engineering skills to decide what materials you want to use for your tractor. Tractors have a body, a cab where the farmer sits, wheels, an air stack, and headlights so they can be used at night. What could you use to make each of these elements?

2. If desired, use the half-gallon milk carton as the body of the tractor and the half-pint carton as the cab, or use your own materials. Next, you'll need to attach the cab to the body of the tractor. Think about whether glue, tape, or another method would work best, and then try it out.

3. After the cab has been attached to the body, color your tractor. You may use paint, markers, or a different method. Be sure to let your decorations dry before moving on to the next step.

4. If desired, use plastic lids and bottle caps for the wheels of your tractor, or use your own materials. Keep in mind that most tractors have smaller tires in the front and bigger tires in the back. Next, you'll need to attach the wheels to the body of the tractor. If you want the tractor to be able to move, how will you attach the wheels so that they can spin?

5. Once the wheels are attached, create the air stack. Trim a paper towel roll to size, or use your own materials. Paint the air stack and let it dry, then figure out the best method to attach it.

6. If desired, the aluminum foil can be cut into circles and attached to the front of the tractor for headlights.

FARM JOURNAL ENTRY

Designing and creating new things can lead to better ways to do something. Write about your experience of making a tractor.

1. *Was there a problem with your initial design that had to be changed? If so, how did you improve on your design?*

2. *Draw a picture of your tractor. Then draw a picture of a tractor in the future.*

CONCLUSION:

You just designed and built a tractor that could be used to pull equipment behind it. You had to use what you had available to make your tractor, just like early farmers had to work with what they had to create tools. Remember, it took hundreds of years for farm tools to develop into what we use today. Throughout history, different people improved the tools. Likewise, it may have taken you more than one try to make the tractor functional. You may have gone through a period of trial and error to figure out what worked and how you could improve your tractor.

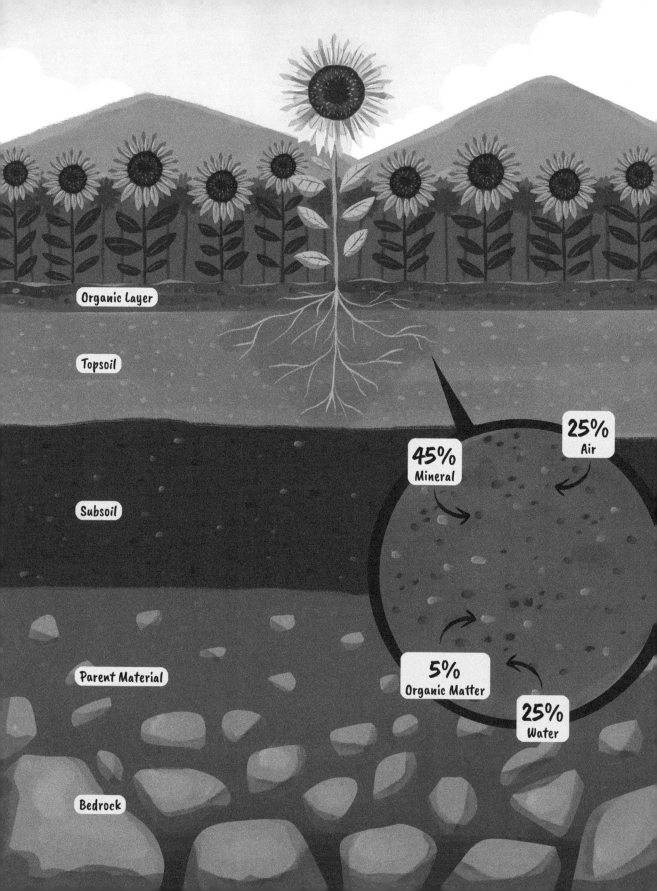

Organic Layer

Topsoil

Subsoil

Parent Material

Bedrock

45% Mineral

25% Air

5% Organic Matter

25% Water

BENEATH THE GROUND

oil is the top layer of Earth. You can kind of think of it as the "skin of the planet," and it's where plants grow. Have you ever wondered why soil helps plants grow? It all comes down to what it's made of.

In this chapter, you'll learn what soil is and why it helps plants grow. You'll also learn about different types of soil, and that different crops are suited to certain soils. Soil also has a life cycle, just like humans, and we'll learn about that, too.

Soil covers much of Earth's land surface and is an important natural resource because plants are rooted in it and get their food, or nutrients, from it. Animals, by comparison, get their nutrients from plants or from other animals that eat plants. In other words, all the energy that plants and animals need to live starts in the soil.

DIFFERENT TYPES OF SOIL

You've just learned that soil is made up of many different things. When all of these elements work together, they provide nutrients for plants, which then provide food for us and other animals. Let's take a closer look at the different materials that make up soil.

Air: Pockets of air are trapped within soil. These pockets provide a place to store water and also provide oxygen to animals that dwell in the soil, such as earthworms, moles, and mites.

Rocks: Rock particles are inorganic material. The word inorganic means that something is not made from anything that was once alive. Rock particles make up approximately half of soil. The particles come from larger rocks, called parent rocks. Just like genes from your parents give you certain characteristics, parent rocks determine what the soil will look like and feel like, as well as what kind of plant life it will support. This is because different rocks contain different minerals, and different plants need different minerals to live.

Soil nutrients: Organic matter provides nutrients in soil. The word organic refers to things or substances that are or once were alive. Organic matter derives from plants and animals. When plants and animals die, they decay, or break down, and their nutrients become available to other organisms living in the soil. For example, leaves fall from trees and break down on the ground over time. As the leaves break down, nutrients that were once stored in them are transferred to the soil. Now the plants and animals that live in the soil take in those nutrients.

Water: Water is needed for soil to sustain plant life. When it rains or when plants are watered by irrigation, water leaches, or seeps, underground. It moves through air pockets in the soil, and plants absorb the water through their roots.

There are many kinds of soil. Different soils form depending on the climate, vegetation, geology, and landscape of an area. Different types of soil help some plants grow better than others. This table provides an overview of a few different types of soil and the plants that grow well in them.

Common Types of Soil

TYPE OF SOIL	DESCRIPTION	CROPS THAT GROW WELL IN IT
Clay	Smallest of the three soil particles; can be seen only with a high-powered microscope; sticky when wet and hard like a brick when dry	Beans, broccoli, cabbages, cauliflower, kale, potatoes, and radishes
Loam	A balanced mixture of sand, silt, and clay; usually made up of 40 percent sand, 40 percent silt, and 20 percent clay; if you increase the sand, it becomes "sandy loam"	Cotton, cucumbers, lettuce, onions, pulse crops (edible seeds from legumes, such as chickpeas, edible beans, lentils, and peas), sugarcane, tomatoes, and wheat
Sand	Biggest soil particle; you can see the individual grains of sand with your eye; feels gritty, weighs the most, and water and air can move easily through it	Vegetable and root crops such as carrots, corn, lettuce, parsnips, potatoes, squash, strawberries, and zucchini
Silt	Medium soil particle, in between sand and clay; individual grains are too small to see with your eye; can feel like flour and is very smooth when you rub it in your hands	Berry bushes, grasses, most flowering plants, and most vegetables and fruit trees

WHICH SOIL DO PLANTS PREFER?

TIME:
30 MINUTES THE FIRST DAY, A FEW MINUTES EACH DAY AFTER THAT FOR OBSERVATION

CATEGORY:
EXPERIMENT, OBSERVATION, PLANTS

MATERIALS:
DIFFERENT TYPES OF SOIL, SUCH AS SAND, POTTING SOIL, AND LOCAL SOIL (3)

CLEAR PLASTIC CUPS (3)

MARKER

RADISH SEEDS

WATER

JOURNAL

TIP

➡ Be sure to keep careful records of what happened to each cup. Date and label each observation in your journal.

Soil types influence the kinds of plants that will grow. This activity encourages you to experiment with several types of soil to see which type will have the fastest-growing radishes. After you gather your materials, predict which soil will produce radishes the quickest.

INSTRUCTIONS

1. First, find three different kinds of soil. Try collecting samples from local areas around your home, like a park or your backyard.

2. Place about 1 cup of each type of soil in three separate cups. Using the marker, carefully label each cup with the type of soil inside.

3. Place three or four radish seeds in the soil of each cup. Be sure to place the seeds in the middle of the cup about ¼ inch deep. Cover the seeds with soil.

4. Place a little bit of water in the cup. If you have a little water mister, that will work great!

5. Record in your journal the date you planted the seeds, the type of soil in each of the cups, and what you observe. Scientists also draw pictures and label them to help with their experiments, so you can, too.

6. Every day, observe your cups and make notes in your journal. Which type of soil sprouted the radish seed the fastest? Add a little water when the soil is dry.

7. You can continue to observe and make notes for as long as you want.

FARM JOURNAL ENTRY

Planting and growing seeds in different types of soil can be a fun way to learn about soil. Respond in your journal to the following questions:

1. *Describe the steps in planting the radish seeds.*

2. *What happened to the radish seeds that grew in the sand?*

3. *What happened to the radish seeds that grew in the potting soil?*

4. *What happened to the radish seeds that grew in soil you used from someplace close to your home?*

5. *What do you think is different about each type of soil you used?*

CONCLUSION:

Planting seeds in different types of soil allows you to see which type of soil grows the best radishes. Not all types of soil grow all types of food. It is a farmer's job to know what type of soil they have and what types of food will grow best in that soil. For example, corn grows best in loamy soil, which is a combination of clay, silt, and sand. Soybeans grow best in loose, well-drained soil.

MINERALS AND NUTRIENTS

Your parents probably tell you to eat your fruits and vegetables. That's because fruits and vegetables have lots of nutrients that help our bodies grow strong and give us lots of energy. Those fruits and vegetables get their nutrients from our soil.

The three main nutrients in our soil are nitrogen, phosphorus, and potassium. Scientists use the chemical symbols N, P, and K to identify each of them, respectively. These nutrients are *primary macronutrients* because plants eat large (macro) amounts of them. *Secondary macronutrients* are calcium, magnesium, and sulfur. Plants also need *micronutrients*, which means they only eat small (micro) amounts to help them grow. These include boron, carbon, chlorine, copper, hydrogen, iron, manganese, molybdenum, nickel, oxygen, and zinc.

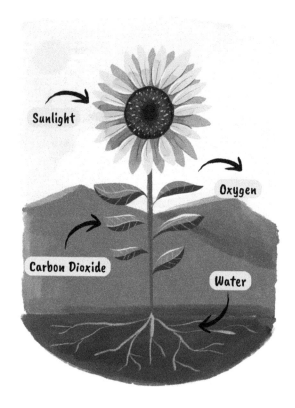

Sunlight

Oxygen

Carbon Dioxide

Water

Let's take a closer look at the six primary and secondary macronutrients.

Calcium: It makes your bones and teeth strong and helps plants build new cells. You can get calcium from milk. When a dairy cow eats grass and other grains, she turns that energy from plants into milk, which provides calcium for your body.

Magnesium: This nutrient helps you fight disease and keeps your nerves and muscles working. Plants need it to make food with photosynthesis.

Nitrogen: You need this nutrient to grow strong, healthy muscles. Plants use it to make proteins, fruits, seeds, and chlorophyll for photosynthesis.

Phosphorus: This nutrient makes your bones and teeth strong, and it gives plants energy to grow strong roots and flowers.

Potassium: This nutrient helps your nerves and muscles work, and it helps plants grow strong stems and fight disease.

Sulfur: Sulfur helps plants make proteins and chlorophyll for photosynthesis. Sulfur also helps you have healthy skin, muscles, and bones.

Photosynthesis is the process that plants use to make food. First, they get energy from the sun. "Photo" means "light," and "synthesis" means "put together." Plants have a pigment inside their leaves called chlorophyll. Chlorophyll gives plants their green color and helps them absorb energy from the sun to make food. Plants also get water and nutrients from the soil. They absorb water and nutrients through their roots and move them up the stem to the leaves, where photosynthesis takes place. This food gives plants energy to grow, and when animals or people eat plants, this stored energy is what helps our bodies work.

Farmers test their soil to make sure that it has the proper amount of nutrients so their crops will grow and be productive. If needed, they add nutrients to the soil in the form of fertilizer to provide the exact amount of nutrients needed for that soil and crop.

Fun Fact

Plants need a total of 17 nutrients to help them grow and develop.

SOIL NUTRIENT TESTING EXPERIMENT

Water —
Clay —
Silt —
Sand —

Soil testing helps farmers know which type of soil they have and whether their soil has the best nutrients to grow crops. If the soil is missing nutrients, farmers adjust it by adding fertilizer. This activity will show you how to test a sample of soil for nitrogen, phosphorus, and potassium levels.

Safety First: *This activity has chemicals in the testing kit that are nontoxic, but you will still need to remember to wash your hands after using them.*

TIME:
1 HOUR, PLUS 2 HOURS TO 1 DAY
OF DOWNTIME

CATEGORY:
EXPERIMENT

MATERIALS:
SOIL (½ CUP)

WATER (2½ CUPS)

1-QUART MASON JAR, OR OTHER
CLEAR LIDDED CONTAINER

SOIL TESTING KIT

INSTRUCTIONS

1. Gather soil from your yard or someplace nearby. Be sure to get your sample from 4 to 6 inches below the surface of the ground.

2. Place the soil and water in the mason jar. Seal the jar and shake it for about 1 minute. This creates a solution of soil and water.

3. Let the soil solution sit for at least 2 hours or overnight. You want the soil to settle to the bottom of the jar with just a small portion of it floating in the water. If the solution is too dark or cloudy, the test won't be as accurate.

4. Test your soil for nitrogen, phosphorus, and potassium with the testing kit according to its directions. Usually, you take three samples of your soil solution (one for each nutrient) with a pipette or an eye dropper, placing one sample in each of three testing cups from the kit. When gathering your sample, be careful not to shake up the jar, and be sure to take a sample from the top where the water is, not near the bottom, which is full of soil. Most kits have colored capsules of testing ingredients, each one a different color for the different nutrients. Carefully open the capsule and pour the powder into the corresponding testing cup. Give each cup a good shake and then let them settle for 5 to 10 minutes.

5. Use the scale from the kit to pick which colors match your soil samples. This tells you if there is none, some, or a lot of the nutrient in your sample.

TIPS

➡ Soil testing kits can be purchased from most garden centers, or online, and cost around $10. Make sure you get a kit that tests for nitrogen (N), phosphorus (P), and potassium (K).

FARM JOURNAL ENTRY

Finding out which nutrients are in your soil and the amount of each nutrient is important so your plants can stay healthy. Use your journal to respond to the following questions:

1. *Which nutrient showed up the most in your soil sample?*

2. *What is soil made of?*

3. *Why is soil important to farmers?*

CONCLUSION:

In this activity, you learned to measure how many nutrients are in soil, which you can't see with your naked eye. However, there are some minerals you can see. When you add water to the soil, shake the jar, and then let the soil settle, you can see the different types of minerals in it. This happens because the heaviest particles (sand) settle first on the bottom of the jar. The next layer is silt because it's made up of medium-size particles. And the last layer to settle on the top is clay, which has the lightest particles of all.

TIPS

➡ Try testing soil from different places and comparing the results. For example, you may get samples from a field near your house, from your garden, or from a nearby wooded area.

THE LIFE CYCLE OF SOIL

Soil starts as rock

Elements cause rock to break down

Lichen forms on rock

Rock breaks down into soil

J ust like you and me, plants and other animals go through a life cycle, a series of changes that occur from the beginning of life to the end. Some life cycles are short. The mayfly, for example, only lives for one day. Other life cycles are longer. Our pet dogs and cats live for 13 to 16 years on average, and a person's average life span is 68 to 73 years. Soil has a life cycle, too, and it's much longer than ours. It can take 500 years for one inch of soil to form!

The study of soil is called pedology. The more scientists know about our soil, the better they can help farmers anticipate problems, manage resources, and create solutions for some of their farming practices. Today, farmers strive to give soil what it needs to stay healthy, which is important because it takes so long to develop. Soil holds the key to our future.

Let's look at the life cycle of soil. Soil begins as rock. Wind and water cause rock to break down over time, and changes in temperature cause rock to expand (make larger) and contract (make smaller), which creates cracks in the rock. Next, plants enter the scene by attaching on bare rock and creeping into the cracks. Lichen is often the first plant that forms on rock. As a lichen's roots expand and grow, it causes the rock to break down. This mixing of organic plants with inorganic rock is the birth of new soil.

The more plant life grows on the rock, the more the plant roots work at breaking it down.

The plants eventually die and become organic matter full of nutrients, which are needed to make the soil healthy. Now, the soil has nutrients, which are broken down further by animals such as earthworms, making the nutrients accessible to new plant life and animals in the soil.

The soil grows deeper as the cycle keeps going. Remember, this process takes many, many years. As soil ages, it becomes more balanced. Nutrients that are taken out by animals and plant life are returned to the soil as other plants and animals die.

Sometimes soil's life cycle can come to a quick end. Soil that has taken hundreds of years to form can be washed away suddenly by floods, events like the Dust Bowl, or volcanic eruptions that cover the soil in lava and ash. Sometimes, soil is lost because people don't protect it from erosion or because they build houses and other buildings on top of it. Farmers and ranchers work hard to maintain healthy soil by using appropriate soil and water conservation practices. They work with scientists to find ways to conserve soil so that it's protected.

Fun Fact

If you like history, research the Dust Bowl of the 1930s. During this period, drought and poor farming practices created destructive dust storms across the Great Plains that damaged agriculture. Farmers did not know then what they know now about taking care of soil. The Dust Bowl led to widespread hunger and poverty.

MOVERS AND SHAKERS UNDERGROUND

TIME:
1 HOUR, THEN 10 MINUTES
FOR OBSERVATION EACH DAY
FOR 2 WEEKS

CATEGORY:
DESIGN AND BUILD, OBSERVATION

MATERIALS:
2-LITER PLASTIC BOTTLE

SCISSORS

TAPE

16-OUNCE PLASTIC WATER
BOTTLE WITH LID, FILLED WITH
ROOM-TEMPERATURE WATER

SAND (1 CUP)

SOIL (2 CUPS)

SPRAY BOTTLE FILLED
WITH WATER

BROWN PAPER BAG, SUCH AS A
GROCERY BAG

EARTHWORMS (2) (YOU CAN
PURCHASE EARTHWORMS FROM
A BAIT SHOP, A GARDEN STORE,
OR ONLINE)

WORM FOOD, SUCH AS
RAW VEGETABLE SCRAPS,
APPLES, MELON RINDS, LAWN
CLIPPINGS, COFFEE GROUNDS,
AND LEAVES THAT ARE CUT UP
INTO SMALL PIECES

PIECE OF CHEESECLOTH

RUBBER BAND

Earthworms live underground in holes or tunnels called burrows. These burrows help get air and water into the soil. Farmers see earthworms as small, living plows that are important for their crops. In this activity, you'll make a habitat, or home, for worms, then observe how they behave to learn more about the ways they break down things and help plants grow.

Safety First: *You will need an adult to carefully cut the top off the 2-liter plastic bottle.*

INSTRUCTIONS

1. Ask an adult to cut the top off the 2-liter plastic bottle with the scissors. Use tape to cover the sharp edge. Put the 16-ounce plastic bottle inside the 2-liter bottle, in its center. (Don't skip this step! It encourages the worms to tunnel in the outer part of the large bottle so you can see them).

2. Place some of the sand in the bottom of the 2-liter bottle, around the small bottle. Place a little of the soil on top of the sand, then add some more sand, then more soil. Continue this process until the bottle is about two-thirds full. Do not pack the soil down, which would make it difficult for the worms to make tunnels. Keep the soil loose.

3. Use the spray bottle to squirt in enough water to make the layers of soil damp but not soggy.

4. Earthworms like a dark environment. Cut a strip of the paper bag the size of the bottle, then tape it around the bottle to keep the light out.

5. Gently place your earthworms on top of the soil.

6. Place some worm food (see Materials) on top of the soil and earthworms. Cover the habitat with the piece of cheesecloth, then secure it with a rubber band.

7. Place the habitat in a cool, dark place before removing the paper. Now you can observe earthworm behavior. Make sure you replenish the habitat with more worm food as it disappears, and don't forget to dampen the soil every few days. Observe the worms for two weeks, then place them in a garden or another suitable area so they can help improve the soil!

FARM JOURNAL ENTRY

Observe what is happening in your habitat, and record it in your journal.

1. *What did the earthworms eat? Which foods did not get eaten?*

2. *Can you see the worms? If so, describe where they are located in the habitat.*

3. *What evidence can you find of worm activity?*

CONCLUSION:

Just like all plants and animals have a life cycle, our soil does, too. Earthworms help in that cycle by breaking down organic matter, like leaves and grasses, into nutrients that plants can use. Their droppings, or "castings," fertilize the soil. You can see them in the soil—they look like churned-up bits of soil. This activity helps you see the role earthworms have in soil's life cycle.

TIPS

➡ **Do not feed** citrus, cooked foods, dairy, garlic, onions, meat, oil/grease, or tomatoes to your worms. Food that is too salty or acidic can kill worms.

Prep the soil

1

Plant the seeds

2

Water the seeds

Sun and water help plants grow

5

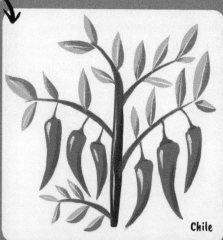
Chile

3

Seeds sprout

4

6

ABOVE THE GROUND

Farmers have learned different techniques to help prepare the land for growing crops. These steps and methods have changed over time as the technology and science of agriculture has improved.

Think about the ways weather affects you every day. What happens when you want to play outside but rain pours down? Most of the time, you have to stay indoors or make other plans. Just as weather can impact your plans, weather can impact farmers' plans, too. That's why farmers have to always think about the weather and how nature affects everything that grows and lives on the farm.

Let's take a look at how crops grow and how weather affects everything we eat.

HOW CROPS GROW

Think about how you have changed since you were a baby. For example, what are some changes you have gone through since you started school? Plants go through different changes and stages, too. Let's take a look at the chile (sometimes called chile pepper) as an example to explain how crops grow.

Chiles start out as seeds planted in soil. Farmers generally plant chile plants between March 1 and April 1. Before farmers plant, they must prepare the soil by plowing (which loosens and turns the soil), disking (breaking up the soil clods), and smoothing before making raised beds for the plants. Chiles grow best in sandy loam soil that is well-drained. Farmers need to irrigate the soil to keep it moist for when seeds are planted. This provides the seeds with the best chance for good growth.

After the seeds are planted, they sprout, or germinate, in 10 to 12 days, depending on the type of chile. During this time, the seeds need a lot of sunlight and water. The plants continue to grow and eventually produce flowers, the flowers are pollinated by insects, and then chiles grow from the pollinated flowers, just like an apple grows from an apple blossom. As they mature, chiles grow edible flesh on the outside and seeds inside, just like other fruits. Chiles start out as green fruits that turn red as they ripen.

Most farmers pick their fields twice, once for green chiles and then again for red chiles. The first green chiles are ready for harvest about 120 days, or four months, after planting.

This usually happens in early August. The red chiles take about 165 days, or five to six months, to grow. These are usually harvested in mid-October.

Most crops planted in the spring, like chiles, mature and are harvested during the fall months. However, annual crops like winter wheat are planted early in the fall and begin growing before going dormant during the winter months. During the winter, the soil stores water from precipitation. Once temperatures start warming up, the water is available to plants as they resume growing.

Once chiles are picked, their life cycle continues as they are used in various foods and products. For example, chiles are used to make natural food colorings. They also contain capsaicin, the stuff in chiles that makes your mouth feel hot, which is a key ingredient in creams and patches that are used for pain relief. Jalapeños are a type of chile that you might eat in various dishes. Dried spices, such as cayenne and paprika, are also made from chiles.

Fun Fact

Even though people call chiles vegetables, they are technically classified as fruits because they contain seeds and originate from the flowering part of the plant.

PLANTING AN EGGSHELL HERB GARDEN

By using eggshells to start your plants, you are using something that is biodegradable, meaning that it will break down naturally over time, and you won't have to remove the shells when you plant the seedlings outside. The eggshells will slowly degrade, putting calcium from the shell into the soil. The shells also serve as pest control, keeping slugs, cutworms, or other insects away from your plants. Herbs are a great way to get started with an eggshell garden, so let's go!

TIME:
1 HOUR

CATEGORY:
DESIGN AND BUILD,
OBSERVATION, PLANTS

MATERIALS:
NEWSPAPERS (OPTIONAL)

SPOON (OPTIONAL)

SEED-STARTING POTTING MIX
(SEE TIPS)

PREPARED EMPTY EGGSHELL
BOTTOMS (SEE SAFETY FIRST),
WASHED AND DRIED WELL (12+)

EGG CARTON (1+)

HERB SEED PACKETS OF CHOICE
(SEE TIPS)

PERMANENT MARKER

SPRAY BOTTLE FILLED
WITH WATER

Safety First: *Ask an adult to prepare the eggshells for you by using a sharp knife to carefully remove the upper third (the pointed end) of the eggshell. Empty the contents and save the yolks and whites for eating! Then ask the adult to use a sharp needle to prick the ends of the eggshells, creating a small hole in each one for drainage. Now you are ready to very carefully wash and dry your eggshell bottoms.*

INSTRUCTIONS

1. If you are planting the seeds indoors, lay out some newspaper to avoid getting soil all over your work area. Use the spoon or your hands to place the potting mix into each eggshell, filling them almost (but not all the way) to the top.

2. Place the seeds into the soil, making sure to follow the directions on the seed packets. Usually four to five seeds will work.

3. Add a little more potting mix to cover the seeds.

4. Use the permanent marker to write the name of the herb on the outside of each shell so that later you will know what you planted.

5. Using the spray bottle, spritz the seeds until they are wet, and place the egg carton in a warm place. Now you are ready to watch your seeds grow!

6. Spritz the seeds every day with the spray bottle. When you see the seeds sprouting (germinating), move the egg carton to a sunny spot. When the sprouts are strong enough to be planted outside, gently crack the eggshells a little before planting them, so that the roots can easily grow out of the shell and spread out in the ground.

FARM JOURNAL ENTRY

Use your journal throughout this activity to record what herbs you planted, the date, and general observations while they are growing.

1. *Draw a sketch of each of the herbs you planted. As your herbs grow, draw a new sketch to show each new stage of growth.*

2. *Which herb sprouted first? Second? Were there some herbs that did not sprout? What do you think caused them not to sprout?*

3. *How will you use your herbs when you have harvested them?*

CONCLUSION:
Farmers follow steps in growing their crops: preparing the soil, planting seeds, watering the seeds, and making sure they grow healthy and can be harvested when they are ready. In this activity you planted seeds in soil, watered the seeds, and took care of them so you would have herbs to eat and use.

TIPS

➡ Make sure you select herbs that work for your area. For example, oregano requires lots of sun. Thyme also loves the sun and can take a little dryness in the soil. Rosemary doesn't mind cold climates. It likes plenty of sun and moist soil.

➡ Try to find soil specifically for growing herbs. It is lighter and drains water well.

UNDERSTANDING YOUR ECOSYSTEM

An ecosystem is a home for different organisms that live together in the same environment. The organisms that live in an ecosystem are well-suited to living there. While some plants and animals can adapt to different or changing ecosystems, many can only live in the specific conditions of one ecosystem.

People, for example, can live in all types of ecosystems. Think about where you live. Do you live near the forest, on the plains, or in the desert? What types of plants are around you, and why do you think they grow well there? What kind of animals live where you do, and how do they interact with the plants? Even if you live in a city, you are part of what's called an urban ecosystem, one shared by plants, animals, humans, and built structures.

Ecosystems can be different sizes and can be marine (ocean or sea), aquatic (all kinds of bodies of water, especially freshwater), or terrestrial (land). Ocean ecosystems are the most common as they cover 75 percent of Earth's surface. Freshwater ecosystems are the rarest, covering only about 2 percent of Earth's surface. Terrestrial ecosystems cover the remainder of Earth, and you may be more familiar with them because they are where people usually live.

There are five main types of terrestrial ecosystems: deserts, forests, grasslands, rain forests, and tundra. Let's take a closer look at each type.

Deserts: Deserts are hot and dry, and the plants that live there have adaptations to survive the harsh environment. For example, desert plants are good at storing water, since water is scarce there. Cacti have a wax coating so water can't escape, and their spines protect them from being someone else's dinner. Coastal deserts have a variety of plants, such as salt bush, rice grass, and black sage. These plants have thick leaves that can absorb and store water whenever it is available.

Deserts

Forests: Forests are characterized by the trees that grow in them. Deciduous forests have trees that lose their leaves seasonally and then grow them back. In the summer, their broad leaves absorb sunlight to make food through photosynthesis. And when the temperature cools, the green pigment (chlorophyll) in the leaves breaks down, and they change color and drop to the ground. Coniferous forests are made up of cone-bearing, needle-leaved evergreen trees. Typically, these trees do not lose their leaves.

Forests

Grasslands: There are many types of grasslands: savannah, prairie, steppe, and more. They are all characterized as being dominated by different types of grasses. In general, these environments allow shorter plants to thrive, but it's hard for taller plants, such as trees, to grow there.

Grasslands

Rain Forests

Tundra

Some plants that might live in these ecosystems include grasses such as wild oats, foxtail, and ryegrass and flowers such as goldenrods, sunflowers, clover, and asters.

Rain forests: Rain forests are forests that get quite a lot of rainfall, which means the plants that live there are adapted to all the rain. For example, most rain forest trees have thin, smooth bark. Unlike other trees, they don't need thick bark to keep them from drying out because rain forests are so wet. Many plants in rain forests have leaf shapes that help water drip off the plant to avoid bacterial and fungus growth. Some of the plants in the rain forest are called *epiphytes*. These plants live on the surface of other plants.

Tundra: Tundra exists in cold environments with short growing seasons. These conditions make it very hard for large plants to live there. Instead, plants like mosses, lichens, and small shrubs thrive on tundra. The plants that live here adapt to the weather by being short and grouping together for protection and to resist winds.

Fun Fact

Tropical rain forests cover less than 3 percent of Earth's area, yet they are home to more than 50 percent of animal species on the planet.

DESIGN AND BUILD A TABLETOP GREENHOUSE

Greenhouses are used to shield crops from excess cold or heat and unwanted pests. They make it possible to grow certain types of crops year-round in different environments, even if they don't normally grow in that environment. In this activity, you will design and build your own greenhouse with the materials suggested. You will then plant lima bean seeds to grow in your greenhouse.

Safety First: *Ask an adult to cut the milk carton for you. If you are using the 8-ounce size, cut just the top off so you have a box container. If you are using a half-gallon size, cut the box almost in half so you have a good size container.*

TIME:
1 HOUR

CATEGORY:
DESIGN AND BUILD,
OBSERVATION, PLANTS

MATERIALS:
JOURNAL

PLASTIC STRAWS (8 TO 12)

8-OUNCE OR HALF-GALLON EMPTY
CARDBOARD MILK CARTON, TOP
CUT OFF (SEE SAFETY FIRST)

MASKING TAPE

SCISSORS

SOIL

LIMA BEAN SEEDS

WATER

PLASTIC WRAP OR A LARGE
ZIP-TOP PLASTIC BAG

INSTRUCTIONS

1. Sketch your greenhouse design in your journal. Think about how you will use the materials you have for the different parts of the greenhouse: straws for the frame, plastic wrap for the walls and roof, and tape to connect things together. How can you use the straws to support the plastic wrap and create clear walls and a clear roof? How will you attach the straws to your milk carton planter? You may need to sketch more than one design before you find one that works.

2. Use the straws to build the frame of the greenhouse, based on your design. If you are using the smaller milk carton, you may want to cut the straws in half. Use the tape to attach the straws to each corner of the milk carton, which is the base of your greenhouse and where you will put the plants. You want them to stick up like poles so you can use the plastic wrap for your frame.

3. Add soil to the milk carton and plant the seeds according to the packet directions.

4. Water the seeds so the soil is damp.

5. Use plastic wrap, which you can cut into pieces and tape to the frame structure, or a large zip-top plastic bag to cover the frame. Make sure to completely seal the milk carton.

FARM JOURNAL ENTRY

Once you have planted the seeds, use your journal to record your observations over the next several weeks of what is happening to your seeds. Note the date your seeds germinated.

1. *Sketch what the plants look like as they grow.*

2. *How long was it from the time you planted the seeds until they germinated?*

3. *What is the purpose of the plastic covering?*

4. *Do you think your seeds would germinate faster if they weren't planted in a greenhouse?*

CONCLUSION:

Your greenhouse is like an ecosystem because it provides light and heat (warmth) to your plants. The soil provides the nutrients the plants will need to grow. The water will condense on the plastic wrap so the seeds will sprout. This lets you grow lima beans at any time of year, even when it would be too cold outside to grow lima beans. Greenhouse nurseries help farmers grow flowers and vegetables year-round.

TIPS

➡ You will want to check your greenhouse to make sure the soil is always damp so the seeds will sprout and continue to grow.

PREDICTING THE WEATHER

Because weather affects crops in many ways, farmers are always preparing for different conditions. They live by the weather and use signs like the color of the sky and animal behavior to predict it.

Some ways of predicting the weather are so common, they've become proverbs, like "red sky at night, shepherds delight." In this example, the sky becomes red when dust and small particles are trapped by high pressure in the atmosphere. This will make the next day dry and pleasant. But if a farmer says, "red sky in the morning, shepherds take warning," this means that the sky is red because a high-pressure system is moving in. And most likely, this will bring wet and windy weather.

Farmers also learn how to predict the weather by reading different cloud types:

Cirrus clouds: These clouds can be seen high in the sky. They are thin and wispy, made out of ice crystals. A blue sky and a few cirrus clouds usually means that it will be a nice day.

Cumulus clouds: These clouds are puffy and look like giant cotton balls. Think of the word "accumulate," which means things pile up, when thinking of cumulus clouds. White fluffy clouds mean no rain, but dark gray clouds mean it will probably rain.

Nimbus clouds: These are the really dark clouds that you see during a thunderstorm with thunder and lightning. They already have rain or snow falling from them.

Stratus clouds: These clouds cover the sky like an enormous blanket. Farmers say that they are a sure sign of rain or snow. Stratus clouds near the ground are called fog.

Animals are also great weather predictors. Sheep and cows will huddle together when a storm is approaching. Birds fly lower to the ground when a storm is coming because the air pressure hurts their ears.

The amount of rain that falls in a year is probably the most important weather-related factor when it comes to farming. If rainfall is low or hail damages the crops, the farmer's yield, or the amount the farmer produces, will be low, creating a shortage of that product. Shortages on farms increase the prices of animal feed and also the food that you and I pay for in the store. This is an example of supply and demand, and it all starts with weather.

Fun Fact

In addition to reading signs from nature, farmers also get weather information from other sources, such as weather balloons, local news stations, satellites, and drones. Now, they can also get information with an app on their phones! This helps them plan ahead.

WIND POWER FARM

TIME:
1 HOUR

CATEGORY:
DESIGN AND BUILD, OBSERVATION

MATERIALS:
RULER

SHEETS OF PAPER (6 TO 8)

SCISSORS

THUMBTACK

STRAWS (6 TO 8)

BRADS (6 TO 8)

PLASTIC BASKET WITH HOLES ON
THE BOTTOM OR A COLANDER

BLOW-DRYER

TIPS

➡ If you don't have access to a blow-dryer, take your wind turbine farm outside to see what happens.

Many farmers grow trees on the edges of their fields to slow down the wind and stir up air. This tactic benefits crops in the field, and wind turbines have a similar effect. Like trees, they mix up the air and slow down wind speeds, delivering more carbon dioxide to crops. Wind turbines can also change the temperature, making nights warmer and days cooler. They reduce dew on leaves, which helps crops avoid diseases that are caused by fungi. In this activity, you use paper and straws to simulate a wind turbine.

Safety First: *You may want an adult to assist you while using the thumbtack.*

INSTRUCTIONS

1. Use the ruler to measure a 6-inch square on each sheet of paper. Use the scissors to cut out the squares. You will have six to eight squares depending on how many wind turbines you want.

2. From each corner of each square, cut toward the center about 3 inches. Do not cut all the way to the center.

3. Using the thumbtack, carefully poke a hole in each corner so that each corner has a hole in it. These will be bent into the middle.

4. Poke a hole in the center of each square. For each square of paper you have, take a straw and poke a hole through one end of it, making sure it goes all the way through.

5. Put one brad through each hole you made in the straws. Take one straw and push the brad through the center of the square of paper. One at a time, take each of the four corners, bend them toward the brad, and put the brad through the corner hole. Now that you have each of the arms of the turbine through the brad, bend the arms of the brad to secure it in place. Repeat this process with the remaining straws and squares of paper.

6. Turn the basket or colander upside down, and place each of the turbines through the holes.

7. Plug in the blow dryer, aim it at the turbines, and turn it on. Use the lowest setting at first to observe how the turbines react. Then try each setting to see what happens. This simulates blasts of air, or wind gusts.

CONCLUSION:

Wind is one type of weather that farmers have to deal with. In this activity, you made wind turbines, which help farmers. As the "wind" from the blow dryer moved the turning blades, you could see how the "turbines" were mixing up the air. This mixing action gets more carbon dioxide to crops, which they need, and helps reduce the amount of dew on leaves, which can lead to crop diseases.

FARM JOURNAL ENTRY

In your journal, respond to the following questions:

1. *Describe how the wind turbines you made move when you turn on the blow-dryer. How did things change when you tried different settings?*

2. *What do you think would happen if you made your wind turbines with larger blades?*

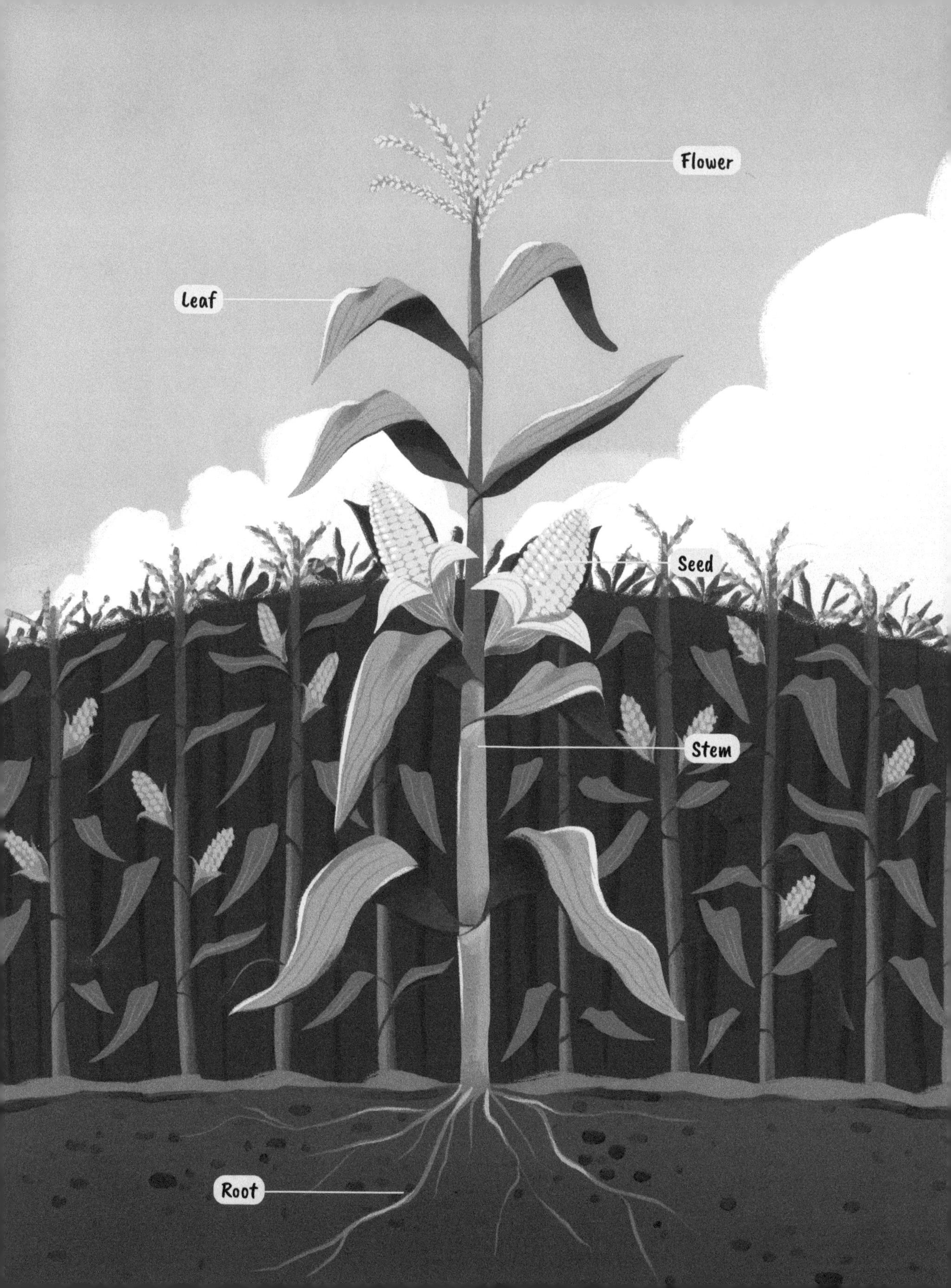
Flower
Leaf
Seed
Stem
Root

KNOW YOUR CROPS

Just like animals are alive, plants are living things, too. The purpose of every plant is to produce its own food so that it can grow, mature, and reproduce. Plants grow from tiny seeds into mature plants that farmers then harvest. We use these plants for food, fiber, fuel, building materials, and more. Plants are kind of like the building blocks of our world. They are an important part of the food web that moves energy to other living organisms when they are eaten. But they also sustain life by producing oxygen that many organisms, including people, need to breathe. In this chapter, we'll take a look at the anatomy—the different parts—of plants and how to take care of them.

THE ANATOMY OF A CROP

ust like the different parts that make up your body, plants have different parts, too, and each has a special function. Let's take a closer look at the anatomy of a crop.

Seeds: Most plants reproduce by making seeds, and since a seed can only produce one plant, plants make a lot of seeds to ensure the survival of their species. A seed contains a young plant, called an embryo, and it usually comes with a food supply and an outer protective coat. The food supply helps the embryo grow before it can get nutrients from the soil, and the outer coat protects it until it can be planted. After a seed eventually sprouts, the parts of the plant, including the roots and stem, develop. Seeds come in many shapes and sizes. People sometimes eat seeds, including peas, nuts, and beans.

Roots: Roots absorb water and nutrients from the soil and help anchor the plant in the soil. They also store nutrients for future use by the plant. People sometimes eat the roots of plants, including radishes, carrots, and potatoes.

Stem: Stems hold the leaves and flowers of the plant and help carry water and nutrients from the roots and leaves. The stem also provides support for the plant. Edible stems include asparagus and kohlrabi.

Leaf: Leaves utilize photosynthesis to make food for the plant, absorb carbon dioxide, and catch sunlight. An opening on the leaf, called a stoma, allows water and air into and out of the plant. Leaves we eat include lettuce, cabbage, and spinach.

Flower: The flower is the reproductive part of a plant that contains pollen and eggs called ovules. Seeds form after pollination. Flowers we eat include cauliflower and broccoli.

Fruit: Fruit is the ripened ovary of a plant that contains the seed. Fruits protect their seeds in either a hard shell or a fleshy pulp. Fruits that we eat include apples, citrus, and bananas.

Most plants develop in similar ways, but there can be some differences. Let's compare the way corn grows to the way potatoes grow.

A corn seed is called a kernel, and when it sprouts, the leaves look like grass. Corn kernels grow into what are called stalks, with a main stem and fat leaves growing up all around it. Corn stalks can reach as high as 15 feet, about the height of two grown men and a toddler standing on top of one another. Once the corn plant is almost fully grown, the male flower appears at the top. This is called a tassel, and it is full of pollen. A little farther down the stalk, one or two ears of corn develop from the female flower with silks sticking out the top of the ear of corn. There is one silk for each kernel of corn, and each ear of corn has about 800 kernels. The silks wait for the pollen to blow in the wind and pollinate them.

On the other hand, potatoes usually grow from other potatoes, not individual seeds. A "seed potato" is a piece that was cut from a larger potato and has several buds, called eyes, on its surface. After the seed potato is planted, these buds will sprout and develop into independent plants that have their own roots and stems. It usually takes several weeks for the main stem and first leaves to grow aboveground. But underground, the root system grows fast by absorbing nutrients in the seed potato until the food supply is used up. The leafy part at the top grows a lot during the first month after planting, and the main stem of the plant stops growing when it produces a flower bud. The leaves will eventually make more food than what the plant needs, and all that extra energy will go down into the thick underground stems, called tubers, where it is stored. We know these tubers as potatoes.

Fun Fact

The average American eats about 124 pounds of potatoes per year.

GROWING RADISHES FROM SEEDS

TIME:
30 MINUTES FOR THE
PLANTING PART

CATEGORY:
OBSERVATION, PLANTS

MATERIALS:
SPOON (OPTIONAL)

10- TO 15-OUNCE CLEAR PLASTIC
CUP, WITH 2 OR 3 DRAINAGE
HOLES IN THE BOTTOM (1+)

POTTING SOIL

RADISH SEEDS

TRAY WITH SIDES

SPRAY BOTTLE FILLED
WITH WATER

TIPS

➡ You may cover the cup(s) with plastic wrap after planting. This creates a green-house effect to speed up the germination process. Once the leaves sprout, remove the plastic wrap.

Planting vegetables from seeds can be a fun way to grow your own food and to observe the different stages a plant goes through as it grows.

Safety First: *Ask an adult to poke two or three drainage holes in the bottom of each plastic cup for you.*

INSTRUCTIONS

1. Use the spoon or your hands to fill the cup(s) half-way with potting soil. Feel free to plant in as many cups as you'd like.

2. Plant the radish seeds ½ inch deep into the soil and about 1 inch apart from one another.

3. Place the cups in the tray. Use the spray bottle to moisten the soil and the seeds. The tray will catch any water that drains through the cups.

4. Place the container in a sunny spot. Now you are ready to observe the seeds as they grow!

TIPS

→ Radishes need plenty of water to make root bulbs plump. The soil should stay moist but not overwatered. Watering every other day should be fine.

CONCLUSION:

All seeds go through stages of growth. In this activity, you started with a radish seed. After about three to four days, the seed grew into a seedling, or sprout. A seedling is a young plant that grows out of a seed. It is much smaller than the adult plant but looks about the same, with a stem and green leaves. As the plant grew, you noticed little red bulbs, which are the root of the radish and the part you eat.

FARM JOURNAL ENTRY

In your journal, respond to the following:

1. *Draw and label the parts of your radish and its stages of growth, including the seed, leaves, stem, and root.*

2. *Are radishes fruits or vegetables? Why?*

THE MOST POPULAR CROPS

If you take a drive across the United States, you will see crops growing in every state. Did you ever wonder what the most popular crops that farmers grow are? The following five crops account for 90 percent of the harvested land in the United States.

Corn: Corn is considered a type of grain. It is used to feed livestock and to make foods like cereal, corn chips, and corn bread. It's also used to make ethanol, which is a blend of gasoline and alcohol that can be used in motor vehicles. There are over 4,200 uses for corn and more being discovered all the time! Corn is the number one crop grown in the United States and the second largest crop in the whole world. There are almost 92 million acres of corn planted in the United States alone. That's about 69 million football fields!

Cotton: Cotton is mainly used as a fiber for clothing. One bale of cotton weighs about 480 pounds and can make 680,000 cotton balls, 215 pairs of jeans, or 6.5 million cotton swabs. China, the United States, India, and Pakistan are the leading producers of the world's cotton. Cotton seed is also used in livestock feed.

Corn

Cotton

Hay: Hay is a forage crop that is dried and then collected and compacted into bales that are more manageable for transporting. Hay is mainly used to feed livestock during the winter months, when the pasture grass is not growing. Alfalfa and grass hay are the most common types in the United States.

Soybeans: Soybeans are an oilseed like sunflowers, peanuts, cotton, and flax. Soybeans are used to make animal feed, biodiesel for vehicles, and hundreds of items at the grocery store, like milk alternatives, tofu, salad dressings, chewing gum, candles, and even crayons! Soybeans were first cultivated in northern China and brought to the United States in the early 1800s.

Wheat: Wheat is grain that is mostly used to make food for people, like bread, pasta, and cereal. Your favorite pizza is made with dough made from wheat flour. Last year, the United States made 3 billion pizzas—that's about 40 pizzas for each person!

Hay

Soybeans

Fun Fact

One acre of soybeans can produce 82,368 crayons.

Wheat

MAKING BIODEGRADABLE BIOPLASTIC

TIME:
30 MINUTES

CATEGORY:
EXPERIMENT

MATERIALS:
CORNSTARCH (1 TABLESPOON)

WATER (1 TABLESPOON)

CORN OIL (2 DROPS)

FOOD COLORING OF CHOICE
(2 TO 3 DROPS)

ZIP-TOP PLASTIC BAG

MICROWAVE

TIPS

➡ Try this activity again, mixing two different primary colors (blue, red, and yellow are the primary colors) of food coloring into the mixture. What happens when you do this?

Plastic is made from petroleum, a fossil fuel that is a nonrenewable resource. In this activity you will make a bioplastic from cornstarch and corn oil, products made from corn, which is a renewable resource. When bioplastics are exposed to the environment, they break down into nontoxic compounds so they are biodegradable, meaning they will decompose into natural elements over time. This activity just makes a small amount so you can see what bioplastic is.

INSTRUCTIONS

1. Place the cornstarch, water, corn oil, and food coloring into the plastic bag. Seal the bag and gently squish it to mix everything together.

2. Open the bag a little bit so steam can escape. Carefully place the bag into the microwave, propping it upright, and microwave the mixture for 20 seconds. Be careful when removing the bag: It will be hot!

3. Let the mixture cool for several minutes, then take it out of the bag and knead it with your hands. Form it into a ball. What does it feel like?

CONCLUSION:

Corn is one of the most widely used crops. In this activity you used corn products to make a type of plastic. The most popular crops a farmer grows are not just food that you and I eat every day but also raw materials for the products we use.

FARM JOURNAL ENTRY

Use your journal to reflect on the following questions:

1. Describe the mixture in your bag after adding the four ingredients. How does it feel when you slowly squish the bag?

2. What does your new mixture look like after you microwave it?

3. What does it feel like after the mixture cools?

4. What could you use your bioplastic for?

TAKING CARE OF CROPS

What are some essential things that you need in order to survive? You probably named food, shelter, water, and the sun. Plants need these same things, and it's the farmer's job to take care of them. The better a farmer takes care of their crops, the higher the yield, or output, the farmer gets and the better quality of food for people to eat. Let's take a close look at what plants need to thrive.

Potatoes

Air and sunlight: These are essential to plant growth and part of the elements that mother nature provides for all of us. Plants need carbon dioxide from the air and sunlight to produce food through photosynthesis.

Insects: Some insects are beneficial to plants. Most of the crops that are used to make food for humans depend, at least in part, on pollinators. Pollination ensures the production of seeds and is necessary for many plants to reproduce.

Nutrients: Very much like the vitamins and minerals that we eat, nutrients from the soil give plants the energy that they need to grow. Early farmers planted the same crops, year after year, without changing fields. But this would use up the nutrients. Modern farmers discovered that they can add nutrients back to depleted soil. To do this, they add animal waste (manure), decayed plants, and fertilizer to the soil so it contains the nutrients they need to grow more crops. They also practice crop rotation, where one year they may plant a field with oats and the next year they'll plant that field with a different crop that uses different nutrients from the soil.

Soil: Soil is vital to a farmer producing quality food. Farmers do many things to help protect the soil. Erosion is a big problem with our soil, so farmers use terracing, where they create levels in the field to prevent erosion. Terracing reduces the steepness of the hill, making it harder for topsoil to wash away. No-tillage plowing is when a farmer only takes the fruits or vegetables from the crop and leaves the stalks and roots to rot in place, putting nutrients back into the soil and providing ground cover, which helps prevent erosion.

Water: Water is essential for all life, and farmers use a variety of irrigation systems to get water to plants. Surface irrigation relies on gravity to flow water over the soil, while sprinkler irrigation sprays water onto plants through pipes.

FARMER'S SOIL BABY

TIME:
30 MINUTES

CATEGORY:
CREATIVE, OBSERVATION, PLANTS

MATERIALS:
GRASS SEED (1 TO 2 TEASPOONS)

KNEE-HIGH NYLON STOCKING

POTTING SOIL (2 CUPS)

MARKER OR CRAFT SUPPLIES,
SUCH AS POM-POMS,
GOOGLY EYES, AND PIPE
CLEANERS (OPTIONAL)

10- TO 12-OUNCE PLASTIC CUP

WATER

SCISSORS (OPTIONAL)

TIPS

➡ Instead of making a face on your soil baby, take a picture of just your face, print it, and glue it onto the side of the cup. This makes a fun soil kid!

Just like parents take care of children, farmers care for the crops they are growing. When you take care of plants, you need to make sure they have nutrients from soil, water, sunlight, and air. This activity will allow you to make a soil baby using grass seed and to care for it while it grows. Your soil baby will grow "hair" from its head in the form of grass.

INSTRUCTIONS

1. Place the grass seed in the toe of the nylon stocking—this is where the grass will sprout and grow. The toe of the stocking will become the top of the soil baby's head.

2. Pour the potting soil into the nylon stocking, covering the grass seed. Pack the soil down and form it into a ball shape, making it the head of the baby. Tie a knot in the stocking right under the ball of soil to secure it.

3. If desired, make a face on the soil baby with the marker or other craft supplies.

4. Fill the cup about two-thirds full with water.

5. Place the soil baby in the cup, with the grass seed on top. The stocking will hang in the water and wick it up to saturate the head of the soil baby.

6. In 10 to 15 days, the grass seed will germinate from the top to look like hair.

7. Add water when you see that the tail of the stocking is no longer soaking up water. As the grass grows, you can cut the grass "hair" and style it as desired.

TIPS

➡ If the tail of the nylon is really long, use scissors to cut part of it off, but be sure to leave it long enough to soak up water.

FARM JOURNAL ENTRY

Use your journal to reflect on the following questions:

1. *How does taking care of your soil baby compare to a farmer taking care of their crops?*

2. *What are some basic things a plant needs to live?*

3. *How are your needs similar to and different from a plant's needs?*

GOOD AND BAD BUGS FOR CROPS

Have you ever thought about what our world would be like without insects? Perhaps we wouldn't have the pesky fly that seems to bother us when we want to rest. Or maybe we wouldn't live in fear of being stung by a bee anymore. But we need insects!

Insects are essential for many ecosystems and perform many important functions. They help build the soil, play a key role in pollination, and some even help farmers by eating other insects that might be destroying their crops. They also help loosen the soil so that air, water, and nutrients can penetrate the roots of plants. Insects turn dead plants and animals into decomposed organic matter by eating them, which helps recycle nutrients back into the soil. Let's take a close look at some of the insects that help out around the farm.

Ants, bees, butterflies, and wasps pollinate flowering crops. Many farmers have their own hives of bees to help pollinate their crops. Other beneficial insects eat pests that harm crops. Dragonflies, ladybugs, praying mantises, and spiders help control aphids and caterpillars, for example.

Then there are some insects that destroy crops. Grasshoppers and corn earworms can do major damage to crops. Cutworms are a type of caterpillar that strips leaves from plants and eats holes in fruit. The tiny flea beetle and the Japanese beetle feed on the leaves and roots of plants. Aphids and spider mites emerge in large numbers that can cover nearly the entire stem and all the leaves of plants. They can also transmit diseases to plants and take important nutrients from them.

Harmful insects can literally consume a whole crop in a day or two if they are not controlled. Farmers help control harmful pests by enlisting the help of the pest's natural enemies, such as the good bugs; rotating crops; applying pesticides to repel harmful bugs and keep their numbers down; and maintaining healthy soil, which discourages some bad insects.

Fun Fact

A mason bee lives an average of four weeks. During that time, she will fill as many nesting tunnels as she can and pollinate flowers while she forages for food to supply her nest.

MAKE A MASON BEE HOUSE

The objective of this activity is to build a mason bee house that will attract mason bees to your yard or garden. Mason bees are beneficial (which means "good") bugs for agriculture, as they pollinate many crops that farmers grow. Mason bees are harmless and don't sting people like honeybees do.

Safety First: *You will need an adult to cut the neck of the bottle off if you are using a plastic soda bottle or to help take off both ends of the can and make sure the edges are not sharp.*

TIME:
30 MINUTES

CATEGORY:
CREATIVE, DESIGN AND BUILD, OBSERVATION

MATERIALS:
SMALL WATERPROOF CONTAINER, SUCH AS A SODA BOTTLE OR A CAN, ENDS REMOVED (SEE SAFETY FIRST)

ACRYLIC PAINTS (OPTIONAL)

PAPER STRAWS OR PAPER BAGS

SCISSORS (OPTIONAL)

PENCIL (OPTIONAL)

TAPE (OPTIONAL)

STRING

INSTRUCTIONS

1. The soda bottle or can is the frame of your bee house. If desired, decorate the frame with the acrylic paints.

2. Fill the frame with paper straws. (You can also make your own paper straws by cutting paper bags into strips that are as tall as your container and four to five inches wide. Use a pencil to roll up the pieces of paper, then use a piece of tape to secure the edge. Put the finished tubes into the container.) Pack the straws tightly enough so that they do not fall out.

3. To make a hanger so you can hang your bee home outside, wrap the string around the center of the bottle, then tie the two loose ends together in a knot. If using a can, have an adult poke two holes in the top, thread the string through, and tie the loose ends together in a knot.

4. Choose a location for your mason bee home. Place it four to seven feet off the ground in a place where it can get the warm sun in the morning and also be protected from wind and rain. Bees need the warm sunlight to fly and also need dry nesting tunnels. Ideally, the house should be firmly fixed to a tree or post. The bees use mud to help seal the bee house, so it's a good idea to have some soil and a little water available to the bees, within about 50 feet.

5. Observe how the bees fly in and out of the house, where they lay their eggs, and how they gather pollen and nectar for their young.

TIPS

➡ Make sure you place your frame within 200 to 300 feet of blossoming plants and trees that are pollen-rich.

FARM JOURNAL ENTRY

Use your journal to reflect on the following questions:

1. *What do you observe the mason bees doing in their home?*

2. *Can you see the sections being created in the tubes? Pollen is placed in the tube, then the female lays the egg, and then she sections the tube off with mud. The female will do this several times in each tube.*

3. *Why are mason bees and other pollinators important?*

CONCLUSION:

You just made a bee house that will attract mason bees, pollinators that help flowers grow. We owe much of our food to bees and other pollinators. Some seeds can only be produced when pollen is transferred from the male plant to the female plant. By making bee houses, you are not only helping bees but also our environment, and you're helping ensure that our food supply continues to grow.

TIPS

➡ Keep your mason bee house in a dry, cool place in winter and bring it out again in spring.

MEET THE FARM ANIMALS

In this chapter, you'll meet some of the animals we typically see on farms. Just like people and plants, animals live in communities and have basic needs. You'll learn about the animals that live on farms, how they grow, and what their purpose or job is on the farm. Did you know, for instance, that pigs are one of the smartest animals on the planet? They learn faster than dogs! Or that it takes only 48 hours for the milk that you drink to go from the farm to the store? It's true! We'll start off with exploring the life cycle of a typical farm animal, then move on to learning about common farm animals and how to take care of them.

5

THE LIFE CYCLE OF A FARM ANIMAL

Just as crops have a life cycle on the farm, so do farm animals. Many farm animals are mammals, just like people, which means their life cycle is similar to our own. Mammals are a group of animals that feed their young with milk from their mothers, have hair or fur, are warm-blooded, and are typically born alive (as opposed to inside eggs). To better understand, let's take a closer look at the life cycle of mammals on the farm.

Cows, sheep, goats, pigs, horses, rabbits, llamas, and alpacas are all mammals. Chickens, turkeys, and ducks also live on farms, but they are aves (birds)—not mammals—because they lay eggs, which means their life cycle starts a little differently.

Baby mammals, such as calves, start out as embryos inside the pregnant mother. The babies grow inside the mother, and this is called the female animal's **gestation period**. Each farm animal has a different gestation period: Female sheep (called ewes) and goats (called does or nannies) are pregnant for five months, female pigs (called gilts and sows) are pregnant for about four months, and female cattle (called heifers and cows) are pregnant for nine months. People are also pregnant for nine months.

After the gestation period, the baby animal is born alive. It nurses from its mom for different periods of time, depending on the type of animal. When the baby no longer needs milk from its mother, it will be weaned—or separated from the mother—and put into a pasture or pen with other weaned animals. At this point, it starts a different feeding plan. The mother is then able to prepare to become pregnant with another baby.

The type of farm animal and the type of farm it is being raised on determine what happens next. Some of the males and females are kept for breeding and continuing the farmer's herd, while others are grown to what is called market size. When they reach market size, they are harvested for the meat you and I eat and the many by-products we get from animals. For example, dairy cows, after they have had a calf, are put into the herd and give us delicious milk, which can also be made into cheese, butter, and other products.

Fun Fact

During her lifetime, a cow will produce about 200,000 glasses of milk. Studies show that cows produce more milk when they listen to music!

POETRY OF AGRICULTURE

TIME:
45 MINUTES

CATEGORY:
CREATIVE

MATERIALS:
FARM ANIMAL BOOKS OR
COMPUTER, FOR RESEARCH

PENCIL

JOURNAL

Georgic is a Greek word that means "relating to agriculture or rural life." The subject of georgic poems is agriculture. In this activity, you will write a poem about a farm animal and its stages of growth and importance on the farm.

INSTRUCTIONS

1. Choose a farm animal that you would like to write a georgic poem about. You may want to look at some farm animal books or do a little research about your favorite farm animal on the computer.

2. In your journal, brainstorm a list of words that pertain to your animal of choice. Use your senses to think of words related to how the animal looks when it is a baby and when it is full-grown. What would the animal smell, see, hear, and do on the farm? The more words you can brainstorm, the better.

3. Choose a format for your poem (see Tips), then write a poem related to the life cycle of your farm animal and its important place on the farm.

4. When you have finished writing your poem, draw a picture of the farm animal.

➡ There are lots of types of poetic forms out there. Here are a few to try out. <u>Haiku</u> have three lines: The first line has five syllables, the second has seven syllables, and the third has five syllables. <u>Acrostic poems</u> use a word that is written down the paper, vertically (instead of across the paper from left to right). Using the single letter on each line to begin that line of poetry, you write words or phrases that begin with those letters. A <u>cinquain</u> is simply a five-lined poem, and some cinquains follow rules similar to those of haiku.

CONCLUSION:

All farm animals have life cycles that take them from babies to adults. Most of the farm animals are similar to you and me because we are mammals. In this activity you used poetry to write about farm animals, their life cycles, and the food and other important products that you and I use every day.

FARM JOURNAL ENTRY

Use your journal to reflect on the following questions:

1. *What images did you create with your poem? Draw them in your journal.*

2. *What message about the farm animal were you trying to express?*

3. *How did you show the animal's stages of growth in your poem?*

THE MOST POPULAR FARM ANIMALS

Cattle

Farmers will tell you that all farm animals have a purpose. For example, many farm animals, such as pigs, are raised for their meat. Others, such as cows and goats, are raised to provide milk and other products. Animals that are raised for their meat are called **livestock**. Not all animals on farms are livestock. Some, such as horses and dogs, serve other purposes, such as helping farmers with their work. Let's meet the most popular farm animals.

Cattle: Cattle are raised on farms for several different reasons. Males are called bulls, and females that have had calves are called cows. **Beef cattle** are raised mainly for meat and other products, such as leather, some medicines, and their manure, which is used for growing crops and fuel. **Dairy cattle** are raised for their milk, which is a popular beverage and can also be used to make other products like ice cream and butter.

Dogs and Cats

Dogs and cats: Dogs and cats are not only good companions to farmers but also work on the farm. They protect livestock from predators and chase away mice and rats. Some dogs are even specially trained to herd sheep and cattle. Border collies and Australian shepherds are two of the most popular breeds of dogs for farmers and ranchers.

Horses

Horses: Horses can help farmers move large numbers of sheep and cattle from one place to another. The rancher rides a horse and uses a rope to catch the cattle so they can be branded or given medical treatment. This is especially important if the rancher is far away from the barn and corrals. The quarter horse is the most popular ranch horse.

Pigs: These animals are a lot like us! Their hearts and organs work in the same ways as ours. Doctors have used pig heart valves to fix human hearts, and pigskin can be used to treat people with bad burns. We also get meat from pigs, such as ham and bacon. Males are called boars, and a female who has given birth is called a sow.

Pigs

Poultry: These domesticated birds are raised for their eggs, meat, and other products. The most popular poultry includes chickens, ducks, and turkeys. Roosters are male chickens, and hens are the females.

Poultry

Sheep: Sheep are mainly raised for their meat and wool. Wool is used for clothing, such as sweaters and hats. Lanolin, which is the natural oil found in sheep's wool, is used in the pharmaceutical (medicine) and cosmetic (makeup) industries. Lanolin can be found in hand lotions, too. Rams are the males of the species, and ewes are the females that have had a lamb.

Sheep

Fun Fact

Scientists believe that the closest living relative to the *Tyrannosaurus rex* is the chicken.

NO-MACHINE ICE CREAM

Dairy cows are raised on farms and usually milked twice a day. Their milk is then processed and ends up as different products in our grocery stores like butter, cheese, and yummy ice cream. In this activity, you can make your own ice cream at home using cow's milk. As you make the ice cream, think about how the milk started on the farm and made it into your refrigerator.

TIME:
30 MINUTES

CATEGORY:
FOOD

MATERIALS:
WHOLE OR 2 PERCENT MILK (1 CUP)

HALF-AND-HALF (1 CUP)

SUGAR (½ CUP)

VANILLA EXTRACT (½ TEASPOON)

1-QUART ZIP-TOP FREEZER BAG

DUCT TAPE

1-GALLON ZIP-TOP FREEZER BAG

CRUSHED ICE

ROCK SALT (¾ CUP)

SMALL TOWEL

CUP AND SPOON

INSTRUCTIONS

1. Put the milk, half-and-half, sugar, and vanilla into the quart bag. Seal the bag and place tape over the opening, making sure the opening is completely covered to avoid any leaks.

2. Put the quart bag inside the gallon bag, and then pack crushed ice around it. Pour rock salt evenly over the ice, and then close the gallon bag, while removing as much air as you can.

3. Wrap the towel around the bag, and shake the bag for 5 to 10 minutes.

4. Open the outer bag and take the inner bag with the ingredients out. The temperature may not be cold enough if the inner bag is still soupy after 10 minutes. Drain the excess water from the outer bag, then add more ice and rock salt. Shake for about 5 more minutes, then check again.

5. Scoop out the ice cream into the cup and enjoy!

FARM JOURNAL ENTRY

Use your journal to reflect on the following questions:

1. *What happened to the liquid when you started shaking the bag?*

2. *What other animals have you seen on farms? What foods or services do they provide for us?*

3. *Draw a picture of your favorite farm animal, and then draw pictures of foods and goods we get from that animal.*

CONCLUSION:

Farm animals provide much of our food supply, as well as other products we use every day. The foods you eat that are not plants come from animals and provide us with essential nutrients that we need. Think about the foods you eat during the day and the farm animals that those foods came from. They all serve a purpose.

TAKING CARE OF FARM ANIMALS

Animals need many of the same things we need: food, water, shelter, cleanliness, and love. It's true that farmers who raise animals are not keeping them for the same reasons you keep your pets. They are raising them to provide people with food and other products. However, that doesn't mean they don't care for the animals; they still need to keep them healthy. Let's take a closer look at how a farmer takes care of farm animals.

Health: Farmers need to keep their animals healthy. This includes making sure they are free from disease and insects. Just like you and me, farm animals sometimes need a visit from a doctor, called a veterinarian. A farmer is always checking for signs of illness: bad eyes, feet, or teeth or even a runny nose! And sometimes the females need help birthing their young.

Food: Feed provides the nutrients animals need and gives them energy. Farm animals are herbivores, meaning they eat plants. Grass is the main plant they eat. In the summer months, many farmers grow forage grasses and forage legumes, which are harvested as silage and hay to feed the animals in the winter months. Farm animals also eat grains, which are high in protein. Plenty of fresh water, air, and sunlight keep animals healthy.

Love: Social needs are important to farm animals. Because they have a herding instinct, they like to hang out in groups. Unlike animals in the wild, farm animals are domesticated animals. They are less stressed living with other members of their species. And, because they are domesticated, they need the farmer to help protect and take care of them.

Shelter: This doesn't mean that all animals need to live in a barn. Most farm animals live outside in big open spaces, on pastures, or out on the range. Sometimes, trees for shade and shelter from severe weather are sufficient. Some farms have three-sided structures for their animals to protect them from the elements. Pigs and poultry need the most protection from the weather and predators. Pigs do not have sweat glands, so on some farms that is why you see pigs in mud, so they can stay cool.

Fun Fact

Pigs are one of the only animals besides humans that can get sunburned!

MAKING DOG BISCUITS

TIME:
1 HOUR

CATEGORY:
FOOD

MATERIALS:
MEDIUM BOWL

MIXING SPOON

BEEF OR CHICKEN BOUILLON
(1 TEASPOON)

HOT WATER (½ CUP)

WHOLE-WHEAT OR ALL-PURPOSE
FLOUR (2½ CUPS)

SALT (1 TEASPOON)

EGG

ROLLING PIN

KNIFE OR BONE-SHAPED
COOKIE CUTTER

BAKING SHEET

WAX PAPER OR COOLING RACK

TIPS

➡ Try adding a banana or ¾ cup of pumpkin puree to the recipe for a differently flavored dog biscuit.

The best way to take care of an animal or person is to feed them. Just like farmers take care of their animals by providing food for them, you can take care of your pet dog by making this yummy treat for them. If you don't own a dog, make this for a friend's or neighbor's pet.

Safety First: *This project involves using hot water and the oven. An adult should help with those parts.*

INSTRUCTIONS

1. Preheat the oven to 350°F.

2. In a medium bowl, dissolve the bouillon in the hot water. Add the flour, salt, and egg, stirring to combine.

3. Knead the dough until it forms a ball, about 3 minutes.

4. Roll out the dough with the rolling pin until it is ½ inch thick.

5. Cut the dough into pieces. You can cut smaller pieces for small dogs and larger pieces for large dogs. Try using a cookie cutter to make fun shapes, like a bone. Place the pieces on a lightly greased baking sheet.

6. Bake for 30 minutes, or until the biscuits are golden brown.

7. Transfer the dog biscuits to a sheet of wax paper or cooling rack to cool until they are hardened.

CONCLUSION:

You just finished making dog biscuits at home to help care for your dog or a friend's dog. Just like pets, all farm animals need special care. The way we take care of our pets is very similar to how a farmer takes care of their livestock. Our animals depend on us to keep them safe and healthy.

FARM JOURNAL ENTRY

Use your journal to reflect on the following questions:

1. *How will the dog biscuit keep a dog healthy?*

2. *Can you name foods that farm animals need?*

3. *Pick a farm animal. Draw a picture and label all of the things they need to stay healthy.*

FROM THE FARM
TO YOUR HOME

Agriculture affects every part of our lives, from the foods we eat to the clothes we wear to the objects in our homes. Understanding where the things you enjoy come from helps you create meaningful connections between farming, food, animals, nature, and your home. This chapter teaches you how to break down different parts of the farming ecosystem and reconnect them with the place that you live.

6

IDENTIFYING FARM FOODS IN YOUR HOME

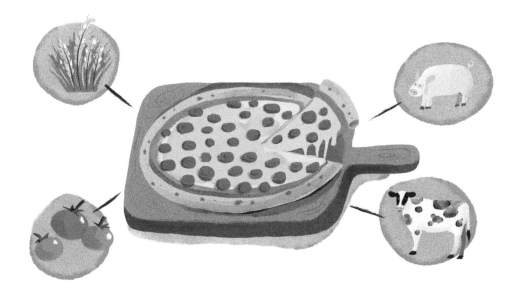

The food that you consume every day comes from either plants or animals. The next time you open your refrigerator, make a list of the foods inside and look up the ingredients to see if you can trace them back to the farm. Let's take a closer look at one of the most popular foods: pizza! Every ingredient in that slice of pizza started on a farm:

Pizza crust: Pizza crust is made from wheat. The seeds of this grain are planted and then harvested, cleaned, and ground into flour. It takes about six months for wheat to go from seed to harvest. Bakeries combine this ingredient with yeast, water, and oil to make the dough for the pizza crust.

Sauce: The sauce on a pizza is made from tomatoes. Tomato seeds are planted and then take about 85 days to ripen into mature plants. After tomatoes are picked, they are carefully packed into boxes and loaded into semitrucks to be transported to grocery stores. Some of the tomatoes are sent to a cannery, where they are processed to make sauces or ketchup.

Cheese: This dairy product is made with milk from cows, goats, sheep, and other animals. After farmers milk the animal, they heat the milk and then quickly cool it off in a process called pasteurizing. This kills bacteria in the milk and makes it safe to store and drink. The milk is then formed into a soft creamy substance called curd, and it is cut into small cubes that are later shaped into blocks or wheels. When we buy cheese in stores, the cheese is already wrapped in plastic and has been aged in cool storing rooms for months.

Pepperoni and sausage: These meats come from pigs. After the pig is butchered, the meat is ground up and mixed with different seasonings to make sausage, pepperoni, salami, and hot dogs. Beef is processed in much the same way, in case you prefer hamburger on your pizza.

Fun Fact

Pepperoni is the most popular pizza topping in the United States. About 36 percent of all pizzas contain pepperoni.

MAKE AN EASY PUMPKIN PIE

TIME:
30 MINUTES

CATEGORY:
FOOD

MATERIALS:
COLD MILK (2 CUPS)

1-GALLON ZIP-TOP FREEZER BAG

4-OUNCE PACKAGE OF INSTANT
VANILLA PUDDING MIX (2)

15-OUNCE CAN
SOLID-PACK PUMPKIN

PUMPKIN PIE SPICE (1 TEASPOON)

GRAHAM CRACKER SQUARES
(20 TO 25)

PLATE OR NAPKIN

SCISSORS

WHIPPED CREAM TOPPING

TIPS

➡ Try this recipe using other spices, such as cinnamon or ground ginger. This is a great afternoon snack to enjoy with friends.

The food you have in your home likely came from the store, but all of that food started on a farm. As you make this pumpkin pie, think about the ingredients in this recipe and trace them back to the farm where they started. Pumpkins are usually harvested in the fall, but this quick and nutritious pie can be made any time of the year.

INSTRUCTIONS

1. Pour the milk into the freezer bag. Add the pudding mix, then seal the bag. Knead the bag with your hands until the mixture is well-blended.

2. Add the canned pumpkin and pumpkin pie spice to the bag. Seal the bag again, while removing as much air as you can. Squeeze and knead the bag until the mixture is well-blended.

3. Arrange the graham cracker squares on a plate or napkin.

4. Cut off one bottom corner of the freezer bag. Squeeze about 2 tablespoons of pie filling carefully onto each cracker square.

5. Top each "pie" with whipped cream topping, and enjoy!

CONCLUSION:

You just made an easy pumpkin pie snack from several ingredients. Every recipe brings farm foods together into one dish. Farmers grow pumpkins in big fields, and then the pumpkins are used in pies, breads, and soups. The milk and whipped topping came from a farmer's dairy cows. Graham crackers are made from graham flour, which is a coarse wheat flour, made from a farmer's field of wheat. The pudding mix is made from sugar, cornstarch, and vanilla, which all came from plants that started on farms.

FARM JOURNAL ENTRY

Use your journal to reflect on the following questions:

1. *List the ingredients in your easy pumpkin pie. What is the source of each of those ingredients?*

2. *Name your top three foods at home. Now, break down each food into its ingredients. Name which farm animal or plant each ingredient came from.*

IDENTIFY FARM PRODUCTS IN YOUR HOME

Just as all of the food you eat comes from farmers, you can't go a day without coming in contact with products from plants and animals that were grown and raised on farms. When a farm animal or crop is used to make something else, the end result is called a by-product. For example, peanut oil is a by-product of peanuts.

Plants have many by-products that we use every day, as do livestock. There's a saying that everything in livestock but the "moo" and the "oink" can be used for by-products. Let's take a look at the by-products that come from popular crops and livestock.

Beef hide is used to make baseball gloves

Beef: Beef hide and hair are used to make shoes, luggage, purses, baseball gloves, footballs, violin strings, wallets, and car upholstery. Bones and horns are used to make piano keys, knife handles, vitamin capsules, lipstick, and combs. The glands and organs can be made into asphalt, cosmetics, fertilizer, insulation, medicines, insulin for diabetes patients, paint, soap, and tires. Collagen is an ingredient in gelatin that comes from cattle and is also used to make candies, gums, and marshmallows.

Cotton is used in printing money

Cotton: Cotton is much more than just a fiber source. Besides jeans, bed sheets, bath towels, and socks, cotton is made into the paper used in printing money as well as other apparel and home textiles. The seeds are also pressed and turned into cottonseed oil for cooking, cosmetics, and soap. Linters, the fuzz left after processing cotton, are often used for medical supplies and cotton balls and swabs. You can also find cotton by-products in ice cream, wallpaper, hot dog casings, and baseballs!

Corn: We eat ripe sweet corn, but the kernels of some corn make the snack popcorn, and dent corn is used for animal feed and processed into cornstarch. Cornstarch is used to make baby food, glue, deodorant, batteries, rubber tires, and spark plugs. Corn syrup is used in sodas, fireworks, and adhesives. Dextrose is used not only in bakery goods and fruit juices but also in antibiotics and oil. Ethanol is used for fuel and hand sanitizer and also in the corn-based plastics used to make bags, containers, and cups. Some other products that are made from corn include toothpaste, gum, shampoo, cosmetics, envelopes, and glass cleaner, which has at least five different ingredients derived from corn.

Soybeans: Soybeans are used in biodiesel fuel for diesel engines, many brands of home carpet and car upholstery, some of the plastic in cars, many cleaners, paints, candles, soy ink, and crayons. Soy foam can be used in coolers, refrigerators, and shoes.

Swine or pigs: A pig's heart valves are used to replace damaged or sick human heart valves, and the skin from hogs can be used to help treat burn victims. Pig by-products are also in insulin, other medicines, buttons, glue, antifreeze, crayons, chalk, and water filters.

Toothpaste has ingredients derived from corn

Soybeans are used in candles

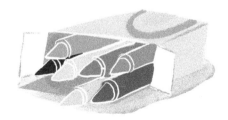

Pig by-products are used to make crayons

BY-PRODUCTS FARM CHARM

TIME:
30 MINUTES

CATEGORY:
CREATIVE

MATERIALS:
PIPE CLEANER (ANY COLOR)

WHITE BEAD

YELLOW BEADS (2)

GREEN BEAD

BROWN BEAD

PINK BEAD

REDDISH BROWN OR BLACK BEAD

BLACK BEAD

TIPS

➡ The pipe cleaner and beads can be purchased at any craft store.

➡ Design a different bracelet with other colored beads to represent other plants and animals of your choice.

The farm is the source of the food that we eat and other products we use every day. The farm charm is a beaded bracelet that you can wear to help remind you of the importance of farms in our lives and how many products started there.

INSTRUCTIONS

1. Take the pipe cleaner and place each of the colored beads onto the pipe cleaner. You can place the beads in the order of your choice.

2. Each bead represents a farm plant or animal. White represents cotton, yellow represents corn and wheat, green represents soybeans, brown represents forests, pink represents pigs, reddish brown or black represents beef cattle, and black represents sheep.

3. As you place each bead onto the pipe cleaner, think about the products in your home that come from that plant or animal.

4. Close the pipe cleaner into a circle, then twist the two ends together. Place the bracelet on your wrist.

FARM JOURNAL ENTRY

Use your journal to reflect on the following question:

1. *Draw six columns on a sheet of paper in your journal. Label the columns with these names of plants and animals that are grown on farms (which are also called* agricultural commodities*): Corn, Cotton, Cows, Pigs, Soybeans, and Timber. Write the names of items in your bedroom under the agricultural commodity from which they could have been made.*

CONCLUSION:

We use many products every day that come from the farm. Each one of the beads on your bracelet represents a plant or animal that was raised on a farm and all of the many products that are made from that plant or animal. Think about this as you go through your day and ask yourself, "Is this something that came from a plant or animal that a farmer raised?" It might only be one ingredient in the product, such as the cornstarch used in batteries, but that one ingredient started on a farm, and batteries couldn't be made without it.

AGRICULTURE BRINGS THE WORLD TOGETHER

Think about the foods that are your favorites to eat. Did you think of burgers and French fries, chocolate ice cream, or pineapple on pizza? Many of these foods are popular in America today, but 500 years ago, depending on where you lived, many people did not have pineapples, chocolate, potatoes, or beef! Back then, food supply chains were different. For example, in North America, people had potatoes, but they did not have cows for beef.

Many of the foods we eat today originally came from different parts of the world. People from different cultures brought many types of delicious foods to the United States. Today, US farmers grow many of these foods because of the different climates and soil, and with the aid of farm machines that help them make more food than ever before. Let's take a look at these tables to see where some of your favorite farm animals and crops came from.

Livestock from Around the World		
ANIMAL	PLACE OF ORIGIN	BIGGEST PRODUCERS TODAY
Cattle	Southwest Asia	India, Brazil, United States
Chicken	China, India	United States, China
Eggs	Southeast Asia	China, United States
Hogs	Southwest Asia	China, Germany, United States
Horses	Ukraine	United States, Mexico, China
Sheep	Middle East, Central Asia	China, Australia, India

Crops from Around the World

CROP	PLACE OF ORIGIN	BIGGEST PRODUCERS TODAY
Bananas	Malaysia (Asia)	Asia, South America
Carrots	Afghanistan (South Asia)	China, United States
Coffee beans	Ethiopia (Africa)	Africa, Asia, South and Central America
Cotton seeds	South Asia	Brazil, India, United States
Grapes	Turkey	France, Italy, United States
Olives	Mediterranean region	Mediterranean region, North Africa, South America
Oranges	Pakistan	Brazil, China, United States
Rice	India	Asia
Soybeans	Northeast China	Argentina, Brazil, United States
Sugarcane	India	Brazil, China, India
Watermelon	Africa	China, Turkey
Wheat	Turkey	China, India, Russia

REGROW FOOD FROM SCRAPS

TIME:
30 MINUTES, THEN A FEW MINUTES
FOR OBSERVATION EACH DAY

CATEGORY:
OBSERVATION, PLANTS

MATERIALS:
AVOCADO, PINEAPPLE, OR POTATO

TOOTHPICKS

TOWEL

WIDEMOUTHED JAR,
GLASS, OR BOWL

WATER

KNIFE

PLANTER AND SOIL

Farmers are great at recycling our food. They have learned that some crops, originally grown in other countries, can be regrown from scraps of that crop. Choose one or more of the foods listed here that originally grew outside the United States and regrow them from scraps.

INSTRUCTIONS

1. To regrow an avocado: Clean off the avocado's pit and rinse it under cold water. Towel-dry the pit, then, with the point-side up, push four evenly spaced toothpicks into the middle of the pit. Fill a jar or glass (even a cut-off 2-liter plastic bottle will work) with enough water so that, when balanced by the toothpicks on the opening, the pit will be halfway submerged. With the point-side up, place the pit into the container using the toothpicks to balance it on top. Put the container in a sunny area and change the water every 1 to 2 days. After 3 to 6 weeks, the top of the pit should begin to split open. It will take about 3 months for your tree to be around 7 to 8 inches tall, and then you can replant it in a 10-inch pot.

2. To regrow a pineapple: Have an adult help you slice off the top of the pineapple (the part with the crown, or leaves, on it). Hold the sliced-off top by the leaves and, holding the fruit part with your other hand, twist off the leafy part of the pineapple and eat or discard the fruit part. Then peel back the leaves around the base of the leaf crown and strip off any leaves around the bottom so some of the stem is exposed. Without damaging the stem, remove any excess fruit to keep it from rotting or possibly killing the plant. Poke 3 to 4 toothpicks into the pineapple base, right above the area where the leaves were peeled back. Use the toothpicks to hold up the pineapple top over your jar. Add enough water to cover the base of the pineapple top in the container. Place it in a sunny spot and change the water every 2 days. Roots should form after a week, and the green leaves will also be longer. Plant the pineapple in a pot as soon as the roots are fully formed. Keep it in a sunny spot and water it regularly. A pineapple tree can take up to 2 years to bear fruit.

3. To regrow potatoes: Cut the potato into two pieces, and make sure each half has at least one or two eyes. Let the pieces sit overnight at room temperature until the cut parts are dry. Place the pieces 1 foot apart in a planter with about 8 inches of soil, with the cut-side facing down. Keep the soil wet, and if the potato is exposed, cover it with more soil. After a few days, green sprouts will appear. Eventually the potato plant will die, sometimes after flowering. Check to see if the potatoes are big enough to eat. If they are still small, leave them for a few days. You can harvest potatoes for several months.

CONCLUSION:

Some plants regrow from the root system, while others need to grow from a seed. Some crops will only grow with the right soil mixture, lighting, temperatures, and climate. Farmers need to know the best conditions for the crops they grow.

TIPS

➡ There are many more foods that can be regrown. Experiment with some of your other favorite plants and see what happens.

FARM JOURNAL ENTRY

Use your journal to reflect on the following questions: ▼

1. *Why is regrowing food important?*

2. *What did you observe about your plant as it was regrowing?*

TAKE CARE OF YOURSELF AND THE PLANET

J ust like we need to do things to take care of our bodies—such as eating healthy food, practicing good hygiene, and getting plenty of exercise—farmers need to do certain things to take care of their plants and animals. This ensures that the quality of their products will be good, and it also ensures that they will be able to grow our food for generations to come. Today's farmers and scientists are also working on ways to use farming to help protect the environment. Agriculture is the key to keeping both ourselves and the planet alive.

Successfully growing crops depends on three things: the seeds, the soil, and what goes into the soil, such as water and nutrients. Crops flourish in soil that is full of nutrients. Farmers use manure, which is animal waste, and compost, which is rotted plant matter, to help enrich their soil. By planting certain crops, such as soybeans, farmers can put essential nitrogen back into the soil. Man-made fertilizers contain all the mineral nutrients needed in different types of soil.

Farmers also rotate their crops, meaning that the soil is not planted with the same crop year after year. Different plants take different nutrients out of the soil, so if you plant the same thing over and over, some nutrients will be depleted, leaving the soil unhealthy. Rotating crops helps prevent this. No-till, a type of conservation tillage, is another way that farmers are protecting the soil by not working the ground as much.

Some fruits and vegetables can be grown successfully by just using water with key nutrients added. This is called hydroponics, and it is a system that is becoming more widely used. With this system, food can be grown vertically in "hydroponic towers," which means you can grow more food in less space.

Fun Fact

Every year, hundreds of thousands of trees are planted on farmland. Farmers plant trees to provide habitat for wildlife while also protecting the soil from wind and their crops from severe weather damage.

Precision agriculture, which uses GPS-based mapping and drone technology for applying pesticides and fertilizer, is used by farmers today to increase their outputs, lower their production costs, and reduce chemical use, which helps the environment.

Today's livestock are more efficient thanks to technology and scientific advancements. Cows now eat 40 percent less feed than 30 years ago to produce 100 pounds of milk! That may seem like a long time to you, but in the history of our food system, that is a drop in the bucket.

CREATE EASY COMPOST

TIME:
30 MINUTES , THEN A FEW
MINUTES EACH DAY FOR 30 DAYS

CATEGORY:
DESIGN AND BUILD, OBSERVATION

MATERIALS:
SOIL

2-LITER PLASTIC BOTTLE,
TOP AND LABEL REMOVED
(SEE SAFETY FIRST)

COMPOSTABLE MATERIAL, SUCH
AS LEAVES, NEWSPAPER, AND
SPOILED/LEFTOVER PRODUCE

SPRAY BOTTLE FILLED
WITH WATER

TAPE

TIPS

➡ Not all organic material can be composted. Some good materials for compost are fruit and vegetable scraps, eggshells, coffee grounds, leaves, newspaper, and coffee filters. Never compost meat, fat, bones, cheese, milk, and oils.

Experts say that Americans throw away enough food to fill a 90,000-seat football stadium every day! Composting is one way that you and I can help the environment. Compost is decomposed organic matter, and this activity will teach you how to make it.

Safety First: *Have an adult cut the top off the 2-liter bottle and help remove its label.*

INSTRUCTIONS

1. Place 2 to 3 centimeters of soil in the bottom of the plastic bottle. Next, place a layer of compostable material. Alternate layers of soil and compost, until the layers almost reach the top of the bottle.

2. Moisten the mixture with water from a spray bottle.

3. Tape the top of the bottle back on and place the bottle in a sunny place.

4. If moisture condenses on the inside of the bottle, remove the top and let it dry out. If the contents are dry, add a little water.

5. Roll the bottle around every day to mix its contents. The compost is ready when it is brown and crumbly, which should take about 30 days.

6. Spread the compost in your garden, or use it like soil to start a container garden.

CONCLUSION:

You just recycled food scraps into compost, which is a nutrient-rich material that you can use to help plants grow. Just as farmers have become more efficient in farming practices and continue to find new and improved ways to ensure that we have food now and in the future, this activity shows how much food waste is created and how much of your food can be saved and reused to reduce your impact on the environment.

FARM JOURNAL ENTRY

Use your journal to reflect on the following questions:

1. *What do you notice happening in your compost as the days and weeks go by?*

2. *How would you describe the compost after a month?*

3. *What can you plant in your finished compost?*

RESOURCES

This book is by no means the complete story of agriculture, and I encourage you to continue to learn more about our food and fiber systems.

BOOKS

Anderson, Susan. 2013. *Soybeans in the Story of Agriculture.* Bedford, Nova Scotia: Northwest Arm Press.

Andrews, Andy. 2014. *The Kid Who Changed the World*. Nashville, TN: Thomas Nelson.

Brisson, Pat. 2018. *Before We Eat: From Farm to Table.* 2nd ed. Thomaston, ME: Tilbury House Publishers.

Butler, Viola. 2020. *Tales of the Dairy Godmother: Chuck's Ice Cream Wish.* Washington, DC: Feeding Minds Press.

Butterworth, Chris. 2011. *How Did That Get in My Lunchbox? The Story of Food.* Somerville, MA: Candlewick Press.

Butterworth, Chris. 2015. *Where Did My Clothes Come From?* Somerville, MA: Candlewick Press.

Cheng, Andrea. 2002. *When the Bees Fly Home.* Thomaston, ME: Tilbury House Publishers.

Darbyshire, Tom. 2009. *Who Grew My Soup?* Morton Grove, IL: Publications International, Ltd.

Detlefsen, Lisl H. 2019. *Right This Very Minute: A Table-to-Farm Book about Food and Farming.* Washington, DC: Feeding Minds Press.

Dufek, Holly. 2015. *A Year on the Farm: With Casey & Friends.* Austin, TX: Octane Press.

Icenoggle, Jodi. 2010. *'Til the Cows Come Home.* Honesdale, PA: Boyds Mills Press.

Mason, Helen. 2013. *Agricultural Inventions: At the Top of the Field.* New York: Crabtree Publishing.

Maurer, Tracy. 2017. *John Deere, That's Who!* New York: Henry Holt and Company.

Mosca, Julia. 2017. *The Girl Who Thought in Pictures: The Story of Dr. Temple Grandin.* Seattle, WA: The Innovation Press.

Peterson, Cris. 1999. *Century Farm: One Hundred Years on a Family Farm.* Honesdale, PA: Boyds Mills Press.

Peterson, Cris. 2019. *Popcorn Country: The Story of America's Favorite Snack*. Honesdale, PA: Boyds Mills Press.

Shores, Erika. 2016. *How Food Gets from Farms to Store Shelves.* North Mankato, MN: Capstone Press.

Siddals, Mary McKenna. 2014. *Compost Stew: An A to Z Recipe for the Earth.* Decorah, IA: Dragonfly Books.

Thomas, Peggy. 2019. *Full of Beans: Henry Ford Grows a Car.* Honesdale, PA: Calkins Creek.

WEBSITES

BestFoodFacts.org
This is a great resource for fact-based information about food from food experts.

AgClassroom.org
Check out National Agriculture in the Classroom's "Student Center" section for virtual farm tours, links for your state's agricultural website, and more.

USDA.gov
This is the website of the United States Department of Agriculture.

AgFoundation.org/projects /my-american-farm
This page of the American Farm Bureau Foundation for Agriculture website is an educational platform with agriculturally themed games. Check out their page "Common Questions About Agriculture" (under "Resources") to find accurate, well-sourced answers to questions you might have about plants and animals on the farm.

Soils4Kids.org
Explore games, experiments, career paths, and more on this website of the Soil Science Society of America.

NutrientsForLife.org/for-students
This is a great website that includes online soil challenges and videos of mining for potassium and phosphorus.

4-H.org
4-H is America's largest youth development organization.

FFA.org
Future Farmers of America is a student organization for older students interested in agriculture and leadership.

ACKNOWLEDGMENTS

I would like to thank my parents, Don and Mary Albert, who inspired me to love agriculture; my husband, Ron, and son, Cooper; and the rest of my family who support me no matter what.

I'd also like to thank my "village" in the ag community—Sue Hoffman, Jessica Jansen, and the rest of the people in the Agriculture in the Classroom organization—for their guidance and wealth of ideas. Thanks to the Deschutes County Farm Bureau, who support my ag literacy endeavors, and to all of my coworkers and students I've had the privilege of working with during my teaching career.

Finally, to all the farmers and ranchers who grow our food and fiber: You are my heroes.

ABOUT THE AUTHOR

Dawn Alexander, MS, lives in Central Oregon and has been an elementary educator for 35 years. She spent most of her youth on a ranch outside of Reno, Nevada, participating in 4-H and the Nevada junior Hereford program. She has actively promoted agriculture literacy and was honored to receive the 2019 Excellence in Teaching about Agriculture Award from the National Agriculture in the Classroom organization. She has also received the Presidential Award for Excellence in Mathematics and Science Teaching. She's been married to her husband, Ron, for 28 years, and they have one son, Cooper.

CPSIA information can be obtained
at www.ICGtesting.com
Printed in the USA
JSHW050252260121
11225JS00002B/2